Serge Frisch, Leopoldo Bleger, Ursula Burkert, Al
Eva Schmid-Gloor, Franziska Ylande.
50 Years of the European Psychoanalytical Federation

The series BIBLIOTHEK DER PSYCHOANALYSE (Library of Psychoanalysis) wishes to create a forum of discussion which stimulates the basic, human and cultural aspects of psychoanalysis as a science and as a clinical theory and practice. The different currents within psychoanalysis will be given space, and the critical dialogue with the neighbouring academic fields will be intensified. So far, the following thematic focuses have developed:

The rediscovery of psychoanalytic classics which have long been out of print – such as the works of Otto Fenichel, Karl Abraham, W. R. D. Fairbairn, Otto Rank and others – will strengthen the common roots of the psychoanalytic movement, which is threatening to split. Another component of the psychoanalytic identity is the treatment of both the person and the works of Sigmund Freud, and of the discussions and conflicts of the psychoanalytic movement's early days.

In the course of the process during which psychoanalysis established itself as a medical-psychological therapy, it neglected its multidisciplinarity regarding the humanities, cultural analysis and politics. By resuming the dialogue with the neighbouring academic fields, the culture-critical and socio-critical heritage of psychoanalysis will be revitalised and advanced.

Psychoanalysis now competes with neighbouring psychotherapeutic methods and with biological psychiatry more than it used to. Being the most sophisticated among the psychotherapeutic methods, psychoanalysis should face an empirical-scientific verification of its procedures and its therapeutical success, but it should also develop its own criteria and concepts to control results. This context also includes the revival of the discussion about the particular scientific-theoretical status of psychoanalysis.

One hundred years after its creation by Sigmund Freud, psychoanalysis faces new challenges which it can only meet by focussing on its critical potential.

BIBLIOTHEK DER PSYCHOANALYSE
EDITED BY HANS-JÜRGEN WIRTH

Serge Frisch, Leopoldo Bleger, Ursula Burkert,
Alexander M. Janssen, Eva Schmid-Gloor,
Franziska Ylander (Eds.)

50 Years of the European Psychoanalytical Federation

With contributions by Jorge Canestri, Serge Frisch,
Alain Gibeault, Han Groen-Prakken, Anne-Marie Sandler &
Eva Schmid-Gloor, Evelyne Sechaud, David Tuckett,
Peter Wegner and Daniel Widlöcher

Psychosozial-Verlag

Bibliographic information
of Die Deutsche Nationalbibliothek (The German Library)
The Deutsche Nationalbibliothek lists this publication
in the Deutsche Nationalbibliografie; detailed bibliographic data
are available in the Internet at http://dnb.d-nb.de.

Original edition
© 2016 Psychosozial-Verlag
E-mail: info@psychosozial-verlag.de
www.psychosozial-verlag.de
Cover: Photomontage – Sigmund Freud in front of the new EPF House
in 35 rue Gérard in Brussels
Cover design & layout based on drafts by Hanspeter Ludwig, Wetzlar
www.imaginary-world.de
ISBN 978-3-8379-2606-4

Content

A Brief Presentation of *Fifty Years of the EPF*

Leopoldo Bleger

To celebrate the fiftieth anniversary of the EPF, we've asked all its former presidents to write a rather personal piece: 'it's the personal voice and experience of each of you that we want to hear' – as we wrote to them in a short letter.

We did not want a commemorative book, but 'rather an opportunity for an outlook and a reflection on the life of Psychoanalysis in Europe, its difficulties, impasses and prospects.'

In effect, presiding over the EPF means assuming a particular role, that of 'an observer of analytic practice in Europe, the training of psychoanalysts, institutional issues and the scientific work. From this observatory position it is possible to perceive both the difficulties and the interest of a sustained discussion between the different currents of psychoanalysis in Europe.'

How should we celebrate the fiftieth anniversary of the founding of the EPF, a founding that one can gauge, in reading Han Groen-Prakken's piece, to what extent is a fabrication of memory?

We have chosen a simple form, namely, a small book that we're giving to all the colleagues who we have the pleasure of welcoming to the Berlin congress.

We wholeheartedly thank all the presidents who've accepted to write, knowing how much some were more than hesitant about the appropriateness of such a piece.

Perhaps there was something unrealistic about our expectations.

We wanted them to give us some perspective, to point out some possible pathways. The 'answer' is that no one knows. Did we think we were consulting an oracle (the oracle of Delphi, perhaps)? There was probably something of this in our request. The answer was clear-cut but not for all that reassuring: it's all in the interpretation that one makes of the expression. We were aware of this, naturally. We're learning it once again: the future remains unwritten. There is no grand destiny. The future is also invented.

What might we find in these pieces? The inevitable will to write one's own history oneself, as if one could confuse what one had wished to do with what one has done. Some pieces could be read as advocacy for a programme, for a vision of psychoanalysis in Europe. One can also read about the intensity of certain disputes and conflicts. History (histories) that concern(s) us relentlessly and sometimes painfully; in other words, they are still alive.

Why so many memory problems concerning the EPF? If the founding act of the EPF was signed in Paris in October 1966, we would have to wait until July 1969 for its 'recognition' by the IPA business meeting in Rome!

Curious memory problems! We hesitate as to the date; we forget the part the IPA played in its creation (unless the two things are related). While several Executives set to work on it, the EPF doesn't have any archives, or at least none worthy of the name. In its way, the EPF *Bulletin* is a replacement; but it was only created in 1972 and we had to wait a few more years still for it to become the *Bulletin* we're familiar with today. Here again, one often forgets that it is entirely accessible on the EPF website, and in three languages. Six thousand copies are printed, probably more than any other psychoanalytic publication (save Freud's works)!

It is perhaps because of these 'memory problems' that we are publishing, in an appendix, a list of all the EPF congresses and presidents. We wanted to add also a list of many other meetings, such as the symposia that took place in the 1980s and '90s. But for this it would have been necessary to collect all the information from the *Bulletins* or from colleagues' memories. We have also decided to republish Han Groen-Prakken's magnificent text on the EPF's creation and its first twenty years, an attempt to remind us of our history.

Why so many memory lapses? Is it that the EPF must now and forever be (re)founded?

Translated from the French by Steven Jaron, Paris

A Historical Survey of the Founding and Development of the EPF[1]

Han Groen-Prakken

1.   Prelude: 1945–1964

The inventory of European psychoanalytic Societies taken directly after World War II tells the story of the almost total destruction of European psychoanalysis. In continental Europe the German Association, whose membership had been reduced from over a hundred to fourteen – chiefly through emigration, but also because analysts were deported and executed – was no longer recognised by the IPA (Brecht et al., 1985, pp. 182–187). Of over one hundred members and candidates of the Viennese Society, only two were left, and from 'the mother of all psychoanalytic Societies, in Vienna, the birthplace of psychoanalysis proper' (Jones, 1938), only August Aichhorn remained, conducting training analyses 'underground' and pioneering the post-war revival (Leupold-Löwenthal, 1982). The Swedish Society, although in a neutral country, lived through six years of scientific isolation (Tamm, 1945). The same must have been true for the Swiss. The Italian Society had almost entirely disappeared, but made great efforts towards recovery immediately after the war (Servadio, 1981).

---

1   [Note from Franziska Ylander] This is a much abbreviated and slightly edited version of Han Groen Prakken's unique and immensely interesting historical survey of the conception and development of the EPF; from the preludes in the late 1940s until the mid 1980s, when it was time to celebrate the 20 years' Jubilee of the established EPF. I recommend everyone with an interest in the historical foundations of the EPF to read Han Groen-Prakken's charming original paper. See: A European organisation for psychoanalysis – why, how and when? in Bulletin 26, 1986, pp. 11–68.

Of the countries that were occupied, only two already had a psychoanalytical Society at the time of occupation, the French and the Dutch. Paradoxically both Societies gained in vitality during and after a period of being officially nonexistent. In France, this was due to the fact that the few analysts who did not emigrate or were not in the army in 1939 (Leuba, Schlumberger, Lacan, Parcheminey, Lagache) made a tremendous effort to keep prohibited psychoanalysis alive by teaching it to psychiatrists in training in various parts of France, with great success and with an influence which spread (Leuba, 1945; Lagache, 1945). In Holland, nearly all the members of the Dutch Society resigned when, in 1941, Jews were barred from membership of Societies. After that, it was too dangerous for the many Jewish analysts to continue with their work. Jeanne Lampl-de Groot and Ritske le Coultre, however, continued analytic training 'underground'. Of both the French and the Dutch Societies one can say that they were 'a psychoanalytic resistance movement', a centre for the freedom of ideas and confidence in the future' (Lagache, 1945).

The British Society was able to continue its activities, although training was reduced to a minimum in a country engaged in the rigours of war. The British Society, however, also had a quite different problem to cope with. In 1927, following the British tradition of offering hospitality to many people from abroad, the British Society accepted Melanie Klein, trained in Budapest and Berlin, as a member, and she soon became a prominent scientist and administrator. Although her ideas certainly met with opposition, there were no serious conflicts until 1938, when Ernest Jones arranged for 38 analysts from Vienna, including Sigmund and Anna Freud, to come to England; all of them were accepted as members of the British Society, and some as training analysts as well. In the following years, the theoretical controversies between Freudians and Kleinians led to many extremely unpleasant exchanges. It required much wisdom, time and hard work to arrive at a solution through which it was possible to do justice to the great creativity of both Melanie Klein and Anna Freud and their respective schools and to the developing Middle Group, among whom were Donald Winnicott and Paula Heimann (King, 1983).

In addition to the above-mentioned Societies, the Belgian Study Group was recognised in 1946 by the IPA.

Such was the state of affairs in 1947, when the Dutch Society, in an urgent longing for international contact, organised a conference of European psychoanalysts in Amsterdam, from 24–26 May. Herman G. Van der Waals was President of the Society and Jeanne Lampl-de Groot and Piet J. van der Leeuw were on the organising committee. During this three-day conference, 18 short papers were presented (by August Aichhorn, Emilio Servadio, Carl Müller-Braunschweig, Willi Hoffer, Sacha Nacht, Imre Hermann, Michael Balint and many others) and four main papers, by Piet van der Waals, Anna Freud, Edward Glover and Jeanne Lampl-de Groot (van der Leeuw, 1947). There were more than 100 participants from 11 European countries including Czechoslovakia.

Although the conference was an obvious success, it bore no fruit in terms of a European reunion. Looking back, this is quite understandable in view of the deplorable state of affairs in most Societies, and the difficulties in travel, which were still considerable. However, from 1949 onwards, the IPA's biennial conferences were resumed, all taking place in Europe at that time.

It was 11 years before a second attempt at a European reunion was made. In the meantime, the European scene had changed, in that there was a new German Psychoanalytical Society and, moreover, a Luso-Spanish and a Danish one. The Hungarian Society was banned by its government in 1949.

At this time (1958), Wilhelm Solms, on the occasion of the 50th anniversary of the Viennese Society, invited a number of analysts from various countries to a meeting. Among them were Ulrich Ehebald, Willi Hoffer, Michael Balint and Piet van der Leeuw. The purpose of this meeting was to consider ways of re-establishing psychoanalysis in Austria and Germany. Both Societies still suffered from a severe shortage of experienced analysts and an inadequate training tradition. Only a few of the emigrants had returned. Most had stayed in their countries of refuge, especially the United States, various South American countries and England. This 1958 Vienna meeting resulted in the institution of the Central European 'Arbeitstagung' which was held from 1959 onwards every two years, and was organised in turn by the Austrians, Germans and Swiss. From 1978 onwards, the Dutch also took part in the organisation; before that they had attended only as guests (van der Leeuw, 1985).

At the same time, the German psychoanalytical institutes, especially in Hamburg and Frankfurt but also in Berlin, invited many emigrant and native analysts from England, France, Sweden, Switzerland, Holland and the USA to take part in their training programme (Brecht et al., 1985).

The French psychoanalysts had long been organising the two-yearly psychoanalytical congresses for Romance-language speakers, attended by analysts from France, Italy, Spain, Portugal, French-speaking Switzerland and Belgium. They introduced the excellent tradition of inviting one member to attend from each of the non-Romance-language Societies, in this way encouraging the promotion of scientific exchange.

Now things started to move fast. At Whitsuntide 1960[2], Piet van der Leeuw and H. A. van der Sterren invited representatives of all European training committees to Amsterdam. This was the first Conference on Training Standards, which was to take place every two years until 1977 and yearly from then on. The second conference was held in 1962 and then the historic third conference in 1964 in London, where the idea of an overall European psychoanalytical organisation was mooted for the first time. (In a letter dated 8 April 1970, Raymond de Saussure writes to L. Rangell that the idea arose at the end of the 1963 Stockholm IPA Congress. I have not found any other reference to the Stockholm Congress.)

2. Preparation: 1964–1965

On *3 and 4 October 1964*, the third Conference of European Training Committees took place in London, under the chairmanship of Piet van der Leeuw. In a summary of the discussions the chairman read the draft Final Statement on Conference Proceedings, of which the following points are of great interest:

1. We did not reach the goal we had in mind in advance of this meeting, as it was set at the previous meeting in Stockholm – which was to come to an agreement, a consensus, on minimal standards.

   ----

7. It is perhaps timely now to advise, from our own emotional experiences in these days, that the Associate Secretary for Europe of the Interna-

---

2   In personal communications from van der Leeuw and Lebovici and in the report on the third Conference on Training, the year 1960 is mentioned. In an Italian abstract (van der Leeuw, 1965, with an introduction by Tolentino), however, the year is given as 1961.

tional Association investigates and eventually organises a meeting at Amsterdam between one or two representatives of each Component Society in Europe – representatives in the top administrative positions in their Societies – to discuss the idea of regional organisation as it is seen in the various Societies, and to ascertain if it is possible to make a start in this direction.

The meeting proposed in point 7 did indeed take place during the 24th IPA Congress in Amsterdam in 1965 and is extensively reported. Pearl King, Associate Secretary of the IPA for Europe, was in the chair. Miss King said that in America there was a Federation of Psychoanalytical Societies and that in Europe a different kind of federation might develop. She mentioned the language problem specific to Europe. She proposed the formation of a small ad hoc committee, assisted by a council composed of consultants from each Society, and suggested that the costs of such a committee should be borne by the European Societies.

In the ensuing discussion William Gillespie asked: 'What do we want the organisation for?' and this elicited quite a number of proposals in regard to possible activities and a possible structure. Was it necessary, it was asked, for every Society to be represented, with the consequence of a large committee of representatives? Or was a small working party to be preferred? How could scientific exchanges best be realised – by shared seminars, by a newsletter or informal journal translated into different languages (Sandler)? The importance of a continuing discussion of training matters was stressed. The proposal for an ad hoc committee and for another meeting of Presidents in the winter to continue with the preparations was given a unanimous vote.

The Ad Hoc Committee was set up (1965) to prepare for the formation of a general European organisation consisting of the presidents or representatives of all European Societies, since part of the preparation clearly involved discussion within the Societies as to the value, disadvantages and opportunities of such an organisation.

To convey my own impressions of the atmosphere of these highly constructive meetings of 30 July 1965, it seemed to me that the officers of the Executive Council of the IPA had a very clear picture of the kind of European policy they wanted. Indeed Piet van der Leeuw told me several times that some kind of European organisation was essential, since the individual

European Societies, divided as they were, whether by language or otherwise – were no match for the large American Psychoanalytical Association and the looser (but at least functioning) Federation of Latin-American Associations (FEPAL, formerly COPAL). At these meetings, however, most European presidents and delegates seemed slightly overwhelmed by the pressure from the IPA. There were a few exceptions who were inspired by the thought of the opportunities such an organisation might offer (Joseph Sandler, Maurice Benassy, Raymond de Saussure, Paul Parin). A few others were enthusiastic but advised caution (Emilio Servadio, Serge Lebovici).

Within the Dutch Society, the President, Jan Thiel, wrote to Maria Montessori on 3 December 1965:

> In the autumn the Society discussed European co-operation. As at other meetings everybody approved in principle, but when the concrete question is raised of how to realize this idea, the discussion becomes vague ...

I think this remark is quite representative of the reactions of most European Societies at that time. One explanation of this fundamental blindness to the vital need for a European organisation that would promote and cherish psychoanalysis could be that many local members, who did not visit conferences and congresses regularly, still lived under the happy illusion that psychoanalysis was a European science and lived in Europe alone. Many people did not seem to realise that with the emigration of the Viennese and German analysts, psychoanalytic science and training were much better organised elsewhere than in Europe, especially in the United States, and were thus of course unavoidably influenced by local culture and thought.

Within the British Society, Joseph Sandler did have some concrete ideas, which were expressed in a letter to Pearl King, dated 11 January 1966:

> It is obviously highly desirable, in the interest of scientific interchange, for French-, German- and English-speaking psychoanalysts to be able to read important contributions originally made in other languages, and this would also have an important effect in unifying European psychoanalysts.

He continued to develop the idea of a yearbook in three languages but was realistic about the cost involved and concluded:

I believe that it is very important that the European Association develops an identity of its own and not simply be an offshoot of the International. A yearbook or journal would do a great deal towards implementing the creation of such an identity ...

The Ad Hoc Committee met in Geneva, on *February 5 and 6, 1966*, 'with Raymond de Saussure in the chair, eleven presidents or representatives from eleven organisations attending (this time there were no representatives from Sweden, Finland or Czechoslovakia). Members of the IPA who also took part in the meeting were Piet van der Leeuw, Pearl King and Maria Montessori.

At the meeting the preference was expressed for a federation rather than an association, a federation being more loosely linked. It was thought that at some future date there might be a progressive development towards an association.

The problem of membership was then discussed. Were the members of the Federation to be the individual members or the Societies? It was agreed that it should be the Societies who were to be the members, but that provision should be made for individual membership, for psychoanalysts from Eastern Europe who had no Society.

The aims and objectives of the Federation – the uniting of all the psychoanalytical Societies of Europe and the promotion of communication and exchange between the Societies – were agreed upon.

It was proposed that the main office of the Federation be sited in Switzerland, as a neutral and multilingual country, but the decision was left open for discussion in the Societies. It was agreed that the Secretariat should be in Switzerland for as long as the President of the Federation resided in Switzerland.

At the Sunday meeting de Saussure gave a clear reminder that the purpose of the meeting was to initiate discussion within the Societies; no firm decisions regarding the Federation would be made until the meeting in Paris in the autumn of 1966. All members of every Society had to be made aware of the great importance of a European Federation. The aims of the Federation at this stage could only be expressed in intentions.

Nobody at this Geneva meeting expressed any misgiving that a European organisation might exert an influence over an individual Society's policy. The masked presence of this feeling becomes clear however from the enormous amount of discussion on the way in which the Societies would be able to vote.

The Societies were obviously far from finding a way of being united, let alone allowing final responsibility for training to be taken out of their hands and given to a European Association.

3.   Foundation: 1966–1969

The founding period of the European Psycho-Analytical Federation extended over nearly three years – from the meeting in Paris *2–3 October 1966*, where the Societies agreed in principle to the formation of a Federation and the Board was chosen, to recognition by the IPA at a business meeting in Rome in 1969. After the Geneva meeting in February 1966, Societies commenced preparations. Maria Montessori expressed concern, on behalf of the IPA, over the considerable differences between the various Societies in the standards of training required for full membership and associate membership. In one Society an associate member was allowed to practise independently, and on becoming a member became a training analyst at the same time; in another Society an associate member was still considered a trainee and, once a member, had to work five full years before being able to become a training analyst.

On 19 September 1966, Raymond de Saussure sent a circular letter to all Presidents of Societies notifying them of a training conference to be held from 29 September to 1 October and announcing as the agenda for 2–3 October 1966:

> *Creation de la Federation Européenne (creation of the European Federation)*
> 1. Discussion of the Constitution
> 2. Election of the Executive Committee
> 3. Membership fees and expenses
> 4. Reports of the Committees appointed in February in Geneva
> 5. Individual proposals

Each Society could send the number of delegates proportionate to its membership. From the minutes of the meeting one can see that 14 Societies were represented: the German, British, Viennese, Belgian, Danish, Luso-Spanish, Finnish, French, Israel, Italian, Paris, Dutch, Swedish and Swiss; in addition the IPA was represented by Piet van der Leeuw, Maria Montessori and Pearl King.

On *2 October 1966, at the Paris Institute*, 187 rue Saint-Jacques, at 9 am, Raymond de Saussure opened the meeting with a brief introduction stating that in general all European psychoanalytical Societies were in favour of the creation of the European Federation. The British had some fears that the Federation would attempt to separate itself from the IPA. After an assurance that this was not the case, the vote for the creation of the European Psycho-Analytical Federation was unanimously carried.

Then the draft Constitution (Pearl King) was discussed word by word and a number of changes made. Essentially the Federation was to consist of the 14 founder-member Societies. Other Societies could apply and their eligibility for membership determined, but only if they were a component Society of the IPA. Direct members of the IPA could belong to the EPF in the same way. The Societies were to pay fees.

The Executive Committee of the Federation would comprise the President, Vice-Presidents, Secretary and Treasurer, and would be elected every two years by the Council of Representatives.

The Publications Committee (report by Sauguet and Montessori) suggested the launching of a bulletin, to be issued in three languages (English, French and German), and of a yearbook – containing a selection of articles and translations from material published in the different European psychoanalytical reviews, and the publication of Strachey's *Glossary* as a basis for scientific work. It was agreed that it would be useful to unite the Inter-Society Exchange Committee and the Publications Committee.

After this the first Executive Committee was elected by the General Assembly: Raymond de Saussure – President; Anna Freud – Honorary President; Evelyne Kestemberg – Secretary; Lois Munro – Treasurer; Jan Thiel, Joseph Sandler, Serge Lebovici and Horst-Eberhard Richter – Vice-Presidents.

Wilhelm Solms was co-opted as Chairman of the European Training Committee.

Thus at this Paris meeting the EPF was founded. There followed a flow of correspondence from de Saussure in his efforts towards developing a viable structure. He found a lawyer to advise on the Constitution, but the actual working out of the Constitution was postponed until the next meeting, on 29 July, in Copenhagen.

During the 1967 IPA Congress in Copenhagen, representatives of the Societies met again to discuss matters relating to the EPF. One of the principal topics at this meeting was the way in which funds were to be spent. It was thought useful for training analysts to be able to visit institutes in other countries to participate in 'Séminaires de perfectionnement'. Moreover it was felt that presidents of small Societies should receive financial support in order to attend the meetings since the cost of travel was too heavy a burden for a small Society to be expected to bear. Then Henri Sauguet presented a detailed plan for a yearbook, to contain papers on specific themes in one language, with full summaries in the other two official languages of the EPF. It would be obligatory for all members of the EPF to take this publication. Joseph Sandler offered to guide students who wanted to establish a European student organisation.

It was at about this time, I think, that problems arose due to the conflict between, on the one hand, the zeal and enthusiasm of a small group of people who worked fervently for the Federation, having at the back of their minds the ultimate goal of transforming the Federation into an Association[3]; and on the other hand the internal worries and preoccupations within the Societies of members who had never thought in terms of European psychoanalysis, who did not feel the need for a European commitment, or were even afraid that the Federation intended to have a say in their local affairs. Where Societies were asked for co-operation on translations, exchanges, etc., the response was often negative or nonexistent.

In this atmosphere a meeting of the Bureau took place, attached to another training conference, on 5 April 1968, in Zurich. The minutes of this meeting are rather brief.

A few comments however will convey something more about this meet-

---

3   I have jumped to this conclusion on the basis of a few letters which de Saussure wrote to the Presidents of the French, the Paris and the Italian Societies, expressing his concern as to the consequences the student revolts of May 1968 might have for psychoanalysis: '... As President of the EPF I am entitled to know exactly ...' (June 22, 1968).

ing. Jan Thiel, at the end of his term as President of the Dutch Society, wrote to his successor Berta van Dantzig-van Amstel:

> I leave to one side the trouble with the Constitution and Byelaws of this Federation: years of fiddling about resulting in a potpourri of Constitutions and Byelaws written in such horrible English that they cannot be used ... It is really incredible what language barriers do in such a small group. (20 June 1968)

So obviously there was not only trouble between the Executive Bureau and the Societies but there were problems of management within the Bureau as well (besides the new friendships that developed, as was obvious in the change from formality to cordiality, and often to expressions of personal interest in many of the letters). From a letter dated 24 June 1969 (from Montessori to de Saussure) it becomes clear that one of the great troubles within the Bureau was the chauvinism of the British, French and Germans.

This state of affairs may have caused considerable discouragement to the Bureau. At any rate there are no extant letters or reports covering the ensuing year, neither references to meetings nor correspondence on new developments.

Time was pressing – the congress in Rome was approaching at which the Federation had to be recognised and the Constitution had to be presented. Montessori attended the meeting on behalf of the IPA.

The exchange programme between English and French candidates had been a failure. A possible reason was thought to be the difficulty experienced by Societies in identifying with the Federation, an impossible goal when they themselves were at times badly integrated. However the Federation had to become active in the scientific field *'sous peine de ne demeurer qu'une organisation formelle discutable et discutée'* (if it was not to remain merely a formal organisation, debatable' and debated upon).

Two resolutions were passed, for an exchange of training analysts between the French and British, and the setting up of a child-analysis workshop, preferably in Holland.

Thought was given to the possibility of a European conference, but it was decided to postpone any decision on this until after Rome, where a meeting would be organised for all European members. An agenda for the Rome meeting was prepared.

In Rome a General Assembly of the EPF was held on 28 July 1969 (Bulletin of the IPA, No. 133, pp. 114–115) at which the Constitution was ratified. At the business meeting of the IPA on 30 July 1969, at the Cavalieri Hilton in Rome, the European Federation was formally approved without reservation and to applause, and Montessori, still Honorary Secretary of the IPA, said: *'This means that the European Federation is now formally established and starts officially to function as from now.'* (Applause).

4.   Founder: Raymond de Saussure

A publication called *Bulletin of Information,* which was never numbered, was produced in a remarkably short time in French and English. De Saussure wrote for it an extensive editorial from which I quote:

> ... Freud was aware of the difficulties and the need to create an International Association of Psychoanalysis, not only to facilitate scientific exchanges, but also in order to be able to maintain a unity of doctrine and method.

De Saussure went on to say that it was becoming more and more difficult for a committee to establish any control over the whole world, adding, 'Also there have gradually been formed associations serving individual Continents (the Association of N. America, Association of S. America, etc.) ... It is for this reason that six years ago the International Association wished to form a European Federation of Psychoanalysis'. De Saussure then described what he saw as typical European problems: the difficult stages of development of the various Societies, the linguistic problem, and the very different financial situations of the individual Societies. He considered it pointless to add another congress to those already in existence. A publication issued in three or four languages was also very difficult to organise. It therefore seemed that the best results would come from inviting delegates from other linguistic groups to participate in congresses. He also felt that summaries of the meetings of other linguistic groups should be published and disseminated. Two other links were firstly the annual conference of representatives of training bodies, and secondly a bulletin, of which this was the first issue.

He then proposed that delegates from committees and teaching bodies in the various European Societies should convene at the end of the year in order to discuss their present and future structures:

> More than ever, our Societies, whatever their form, must endeavour to maintain the psychoanalytical method as unique, and one which must not be confused with the numerous psychotherapies which only borrow certain data from the Freudian method or theory ... It is for this reason that we shall ask the Assembly of the psychoanalytical Federation, at the time of its meeting in Rome, to ratify this meeting of the bodies of our different Societies.

These words, written by Raymond de Saussure while he was suffering from a very painful illness (as appears from letters from Evelyne Kestemberg and Mario Montessori, June 1969), illustrate well what de Saussure stood for and what he wished the Federation to stand for: the safeguarding of psychoanalytic theory, but especially of the classic psychoanalytic method.

A history of the Federation is not complete without some account of this man who, at the age of 71, in 1965 in Amsterdam, took it upon himself to found a European organisation in the face of the resistance from or the lack of interest of the majority of the membership of individual Societies. Loewenstein (1973) writes, referring to their last meeting at the Vienna Congress in 1971, when de Saussure was fatally ill: 'he... seemed to express his determination to stay and perform his duties to the end. Such devotion to his duties as an analyst was characteristic of his personality, it dominated his activities for as long as I knew him' (p. 111).

De Saussure came from Geneva and was descended from a family of scientists of that city. Following his analysis with Freud, and after having worked in Vienna, Berlin and Paris, he practised in Geneva (Solms, 1972). He had produced a quite considerable oeuvre with an emphasis on medical history, psychiatry and psychoanalysis, and which included a book on psychoanalytic method written in 1924. In 1940 he moved to New York but returned to Geneva in 1952. From 1957–1967 he was President of the Swiss Society and from 1957–1961 Vice-President of the IPA.

So he was conversant with the organisation both of the IPA and of the American Association, where he had been a training analyst. Apart from his professional qualities and his organisational skills he seems to have had a great gift for fostering interpersonal or scientific discussions. Although I never met de Saussure, being in my early days of training in 1971, I am repeatedly struck by the degree of respect and good feeling with which people talk of him. His American experience certainly explains why he seems never to have completely abandoned the idea of a European Association, intended in the first place to homogenisse training; his Swiss nationality however must certainly have made the idea of a Federation quite natural to him. The fact that he assisted in founding the Paris Society explains the slightly patronising manner in which he asks them for information after the student revolts of 1968.

I suppose that besides his knowledge of psychoanalysis and his organisational skills, his character, his charm, his way of defusing tensions, his capacity for work and his ability to speak French, English and German were of vital importance in getting the Federation going.

5.   The Geneva Symposium, 1970

Although the official recognition of the EPF did not take more than a few minutes at the Rome Business Meeting, something else certainly did. The proposal of certain Dutch members that the IPA give membership to those who completed a full training in child analysis resulted in a very long and fundamental discussion, but ended – so I have been told – in a real uproar (the minutes mention 'confusion'). The resolution was passed that a committee be appointed to investigate the differences and similarities in adult and child analysis.

At the same time, the young Federation, bearing in mind the advice of the General Assembly of the EPF in Rome (of which the reports are lost) had to decide what to do next.

In October 1969, the Bureau decided to hold a seminar or symposium on child analysis, because of the urgency of this topic. Evelyne Kestemberg made the necessary arrangements. The symposium would deal with a general topic: 'The Role of Child Analysis in Psychoanalytic Training', and would be divided into three sessions to be held on 27–28 June 1970. To open the meeting, papers were to be presented by René Diatkine: 'A review of the present state of the psychoanalysis of children'; Anna Freud: 'Child analysis as a subspeciality of psychoanalysis'; and Hanna Segal: 'The role of child analysis in general psychoanalytic training'

Leo Rangell, then President of the IPA, was very positive about the idea of a symposium and especially about the topic: 'It will be very helpful and productive for all of us to have this complicated issue aired in a scientific discussion, with the emphasis entirely on the principles ... involved from the theoretical, clinical and educational standpoints' (Rangell to Kestemberg, 6 March 1970). By 8 April 1970, de Saussure was able to write to Rangell: 'As this was our first attempt at a concrete project we did not expect more than 25 to 30 participants. To our great surprise and happiness we have received well over 200 registrations representing all the European countries ...'

The conference was an enormous success. In the end all the European countries were represented and there were 258 participants, half of them students. De Saussure in his opening remarks emphasised that the intention was to discuss the problem from a theoretical point of view. No practical decisions were to be taken, but reference was made to the Dutch proposal in Rome in 1969 that the IPA extend its membership to fully trained child analysts. The discussions following the opening papers were lively and free, with participation from the floor such as is seldom seen at international meetings (Kestenberg, 1971).

It was planned to make the European Geneva conference a two-yearly event (*Bulletin of the IPA*, No. 137, p. 117). Unfortunately this never came about. With the final illness of Raymond de Saussure and his death on 29 October 1971, it was brought home once more how much he had been the driving force behind the Federation. The future of the EPP became precarious again.

6.   Survival: 1971–1975

The Bulletin

At the General Assembly on 27 July 1971 in Vienna, Raymond de Saussure resigned because of ill-health. A new Executive Council was elected: President: Wilhelm Solms (Vienna); Vice-Présidents: Peter Hildebrand (London), Serge Lebovici (Paris), R. U. Mekking (Velsen, Holland), Joseph Sandler (London), H. Thomä (Ulm); Treasurer: Lois Munro (London); Secretary: Daniel Widlöcher (Paris).

Apart from the elections, most of the meeting was devoted to changing the Constitution again so as to make explicit the autonomy of the Societies.

23

A few of the existing activities were now made the responsibility of the Federation, the most notable of these being the Standing Conference on Training. Once before, in 1964, the training conference had fostered and strengthened the Federation and it might well be that the resurrection of the Federation from this depressed period was partly due to the high standard of the training conference, where European analysts met regularly.

Then another very important idea was implemented. In all the discussions on possible publications the idea of a yearbook had to be put aside because of the high costs involved (Sandler, 1986). However in 1972, 'Psychoanalysis in Europe' (better known as *Bulletin* 1) was issued for the first time. The first Editor of the *Bulletin* was Peter Hildebrand, assisted by Michael de M'Uzan, Samir Stephanos and Daniel Widlöcher. I quote from Hildebrand's editorial in that first issue:

> The publication of this Bulletin in English, French and German is a new venture ... Our members speak different languages, live under different legal codes and work under very different conditions. Whilst geographically we are close to one another we have far less of a regional identity than our North or South American colleagues. Yet the pace of political and cultural events suggests ... that we Europeans are more in need of mutual understanding than ever before.'

Hildebrand continues to plead the advantages in particular of small conferences and widespread and effective communication.

> We already possess good scientific Journals which are easily available to us all. However, what we do not have is good scientific journalism. Such scientific journalism should have three aims: the identification of ideas and issues of more than local interest; accurate reporting; creative interpreting of such issues. Our task in Psychoanalysis in Europe will be to try and realize these aims ... We shall try to initiate discussion and encourage controversy ... We prefer to know how individual analysts and students feel about questions such as training, relations with other disciplines and the applications of psychoanalysis. (Hildebrand, 1972)

In the same issue, Mekking describes psychoanalysis in Europe as having arrived at a third period in its development. The first period consisted of a group of very enthusiastic analysts in constant struggle against a society that vehemently resisted their analytic insights. In the second period – the heyday of analysis – the treatment process was accepted by society at large and a great many people sought analytic training. The current third period saw society once again rejecting psychoanalysis in favour of the many shorter treatments that give quick relief. Mekking invites the analytical Societies to write about their administrative and scientific development and the way their training has been organised at the different periods.

President Solms raises the question of whether the EPF should have only a representative function or should assume aims and responsibilities of its own. He ventures to suggest that more conferences be held with a narrowly defined topic, such as that of the child analysis symposium in Geneva in 1970. He also questions whether it might be possible to promote analytical activity in the large psychiatric hospitals or in the social services.

Another of the suggested activities for the EPF had been the inter-Society exchanges, several of which were arranged. Whether the EPF took part in their organisation is not quite clear. Probably it was on the initiative of the individual boards of Societies, and then was taken over by the Federation. However, 1971 saw the inauguration of a yearly meeting of fifteen French and fifteen British analysts, in which cases were presented and the considerable differences in technique discussed.

On reading a report by Annie Anzieu (1972), one has the feeling now that such a clinical exchange with its use of a conceptual framework was really fundamental to the creation of a European understanding of the different theoretical schools in the various countries. However, it seems unavoidable that activities of this kind would be rather short-lived, even when they were a success. In the minutes of the Council Meeting of November 1 and 2, 1975, reference is made to the amount of ill-feeling created by this Anglo-French colloquium within the French Societies.

There were also a number of Belgian-Dutch exchanges: nice, small, lively occasions that unfortunately were discontinued after four meetings, probably largely because of the French-Dutch language barrier.

After its beginnings in 1972, the *Bulletin* – or 'Psychoanalysis in Europe' – led a prosperous, unbroken existence, though not without worries. With the publication of the first number, the difficulties involved could begin to be understood: a group of translators had to be organised; an appropriate level – neither purely scientific nor simply informational – had to be found, which had to be of interest to analysts in many countries while retaining the simplicity of an internal bulletin. One possible objective was to have the *Bulletin* serve as a tribune for discussions of general interest, to provide news about European psychoanalytic activities and to make known the thoughts and works of certain analysts who had exercised a wide influence within their own country without being well known elsewhere (Widlöcher, 1973).

With Peter Hildebrand (London) as Editor from 1972–1977, Daniel Widlöcher (Paris) from 1977–1979, and Terttu Eskelinen de Folch (Barcelona) from 1979 on, the *Bulletin* has fulfilled these tasks with increasing success every year and has helped to form the identity of the Federation. Its cover has changed twice, there has been one change of printer, and the number of pages has certainly altered considerably. From the 15-page first issue, it has grown to its present size of usually more than 100 pages.

Although my own impressions of the factors involved in producing the *Bulletin* do not go back beyond 1978, I do not suppose that the present concerns are essentially different from those of the initial period. At every Council Meeting the *Bulletin* is on the agenda. There is a constant worry about the contents. Will the papers be received in time for the translation to be completed before the translator goes on holiday? Another problem of course is the cost – translation, printing and mailing are very costly indeed and the successive editors devoted much time to finding the cheapest possible means of carrying out the work.

In my opinion one can hardly pay sufficient tribute to the three editors and their assistants for the scale of their endeavours, through which they succeeded in shaping the *Bulletin* to their image of what it ought to be: a mirror for European psychoanalytic scientific activities, a vehicle for an exchange of views on the present-day problems our profession has to cope with, an open-ended forum on psychoanalysis in Europe.

Separate mention should be made here of Issue No. 5 in which the Glossary from *The Language of Psychoanalysis* (Laplanche & Pontalis, 1967; 1973) was reprinted as a service to psychoanalysts in Europe. Since that time the shortcomings of this Glossary, apparent when it came into use, have led Joseph Sandler to work on an expanded and altered version. These Glossaries are essential for everybody who reads and writes in different languages.

At the Council Meeting of 2 February 1974, worry was again expressed about the uncertain position of the Federation as between the IPA on the one hand and the Societies on the other. The Federation 'neither exercises nor wishes to exercise power; should this be interpreted as a sign of weakness or as a potential strength?'

Clearly the Federation had great problems in finding itself an identity.

From the minutes of the Council Meeting of 8 June 1974, it is obvious that the IPA was not too clear either about the identity of the Federation, since we find it asking for the assistance of the EPF in the formation of a European subcommittee on 'The Evaluation of Applicants for Psychoanalytic Training'. The Council there realissed that an involvement in personal training was not a task for the Federation, which had explicitly decided not to interfere in training matters.

During the IPA congress in London in 1975, two scientific meetings of the EPF were planned to take place on the 'free Wednesday afternoon' of the congress. Although logistically it made sense to use an IPA gathering for European meetings, in my opinion it had an adverse effect on the efforts to establish a separate identity. The average member or candidate was not always aware of who was the organiser of which meeting and therefore many simply did not realise there was a separate Federation in addition to the IPA.

7. Revival: 1975–1979

The Revised Constitution; the Conferences

The first act of Joseph Sandler's presidency, to appoint Alex Holder as Secretary, was an entirely successful one – certainly from my point of view as the writer of this history. Where the minutes of meetings before 1975 had with few exceptions commented only briefly on the topics discussed; with Alex Holder as Secretary there began a tradition of extensive reporting of the proceedings of Council Meetings, a tradition which has been safeguarded by the subsequent secretaries: Gemma Jappe and Alain Gibeault. It seems to me that these detailed minutes are not only essential for any possible future historian but for contemporary purposes as well. Certainly when a council meets only twice a year for reasons of distance and economy, one cannot over-estimate the value of a written report that refreshes the memory and keeps discussion alive.

Joseph Sandler had of course earned quite a reputation with his work on the Hampstead Index, which he instituted in 1960, with his numerous papers on analytical concepts and frames of reference, written partly in collaboration with Alex Holder. In these activities he had shown his unique talent for clarifying psychoanalytic concepts and for pinpointing confusions arising from the misuse of analytic terms or their use to cover two or three different meanings. In his capacity as President of the Federation, he set about investigating the shortcomings of the Federation, and in 1976 he presented his views to the membership in a Letter to the *Bulletin*.

The first Meeting of Presidents in Brussels in February 1976 certainly served a most useful purpose (Holder, 1976). There was agreement that the main aim of the EPF was to be the fostering of scientific exchanges, and that relatively small and informal meetings and conferences would be more profitable than large congresses. There was agreement too on the unsatisfactory structure of the EPF, which required considerable constitutional changes to be made. The degree of autonomy of the EPF was the most controversial issue.

It was felt that regular meetings with the presidents of Societies – once or twice every year – would do much to improve relations. So improvement in relations was tackled on two fronts at the same time: Conferences were organised (three in the period 1976–1979) and the Council met regularly with the presidents of Societies.

During the 1977 IPA Congress in Jerusalem the General Assembly of the EPF met for the last time under the auspices of the IPA; thereafter the meetings took place at EPF conferences, which of course went a long way towards helping the Federation develop an identity of its own.

The first EPF Conference took place in Aix-en-Provence at the end of August 1976. Mme. Chasseguet headed the Organising Committee. At the Council Meeting in March 1976, it was agreed that what was needed was not 'just another Conference', but that the EPF should try to offer something special, a clinical topic. With this in mind, the theme 'Technical Problems of Interpretation' was decided upon.

There were over 200 participants and the conference was felt to be a great success in spite of inevitable shortcomings, chiefly due to the fact that the conference had been organised at relatively short notice (*Bulletin of the IPA*, No. 143).

The success was so undeniable – even financially, since a slight profit had been made – that at the Meeting of Council and Presidents in February 1977 in London, the second and third conferences were planned, for February 1978 and the autumn of 1979 (Memorandum 9).

The second conference was to be held in Estoril, Portugal.

In the *EPF Bulletin*, No. 13, 1978, containing the Estoril papers, Alex Holder was already announcing the Third Conference of the EPF at the Wembley Conference Centre in London 12–15 October 1979. An important new facility – simultaneous translation into English, French and German – was to be offered. It is clear that the Federation was now developing with great rapidity into an active scientific organisation and that the need for international scientific meetings of moderate size and good quality was great and the time for exploitation ripe.

These three successive conferences contributed enormously to the development of the Federation's own identity (Sandler, 1980). They were also of benefit to the *Bulletin*, which, through the publication of the conference papers, made available important scientific contributions to the people who stayed at home.

With Peter Hildebrand as Editor from 1972–1977, the *Bulletin* became transformed from a 15-page, rather shabby stencilled publication into a representative, well-printed little journal. In 1977 Hildebrand's term of office ended and he was succeeded by Daniel Widlöcher. From his 'Editor's Introduction' it was obvious that it was not the Federation alone but also the *Bulletin* that was developing an identity of its own. In the first issues the Editor's comments were of course tentative as he attempted to define and set the tone of the *Bulletin*. Widlöcher (1978) writes:

> Psychoanalysis in Europe is not a psychoanalytic review like the others, and does not seek to compete with the scientific review ... Our Bulletin should continue to be first and foremost a medium for information and exchange amongst the various European Societies and priority will be given to subjects of general interest concerned with the development of psychoanalytic practice in Europe, the problems posed by psychoanalytic practice in the institutional setting and the social conditions of psychoanalytic practice. It will also serve, as in the past, to give an account of the Federation's activities and the Conferences in particular.

In the Federation, apart from all the activities directed towards the membership, there was also an essential change in the internal structure. At the beginning of this section, I described Sandler's initiative in organising consultative meetings with the presidents of Societies: these meetings took place twice a year from 1976 onwards. The presidents reported and advised but had no vote. Nevertheless these meetings were very fruitful as a link between Federation and Societies.

It became obvious that the structure of a General Assembly composed of delegates – who, incidentally, were attending a congress while not necessarily knowing anything about the Federation or their own Society – was far from satisfactory. These delegates had to elect the Council: people they did not know or had never even heard of. The paradox that the Federation consisted of Societies, but that the membership consists of individuals, made for an inherently confusing structure.

A working committee was therefore set up to revise the Constitution, composed of Janice de Saussure (in the chair), Harald Leupold-Löwenthal of Vienna, and Bo Larsson of Sweden. After an enormous amount of research, countless interviews, plans, reports and discussions, a new Constitution was drafted.

The essential feature of this new Constitution was that only Societies could participate in the Federation, which would no longer allow individual membership. This entailed a change in the composition and powers of the Council of the Federation. It was to be made up of the presidents of all Societies and an Executive Board. Decisions were to be taken by the whole Council, in which every Society was to be represented and had one vote. The Council was to meet twice a year. Between meetings the Executive Board, which was elected by the Council, was to act on behalf of the Federation. Once every two years there was to be a General Assembly for reports and discussion but without voting rights.

This model presented itself as the most realistic and practical solution when the reciprocal benefits became apparent of the stimulus of the Meeting of Presidents on the Federation and vice versa. Fortunately Janice de Saussure and Joseph Sandler had the freshness of vision and the open-mindedness to think of this unconventional, very different and yet logical solution.

The brevity of this report on the revisions to the Constitution in no way reflects the amount of work involved. However once the solution had been envisioned the actual work consisted of minute formulations, which it would be tedious to describe.

In October 1979, at Wembley, Sandler performed the ingenious task of chairing a General Assembly, which, in the act of voting for the new Constitution, lost its voting rights. There were 17 Societies in the Federation and therefore the new Council consisted of 17 Presidents of Societies: the 14 founding Societies of 1966, the new Societies of Madrid and Portugal already mentioned, and the Norwegian Society, recognised anew in 1975, the original Society having been dissolved during the war (Havnegjerde & Helmers, 1977).

8.   Training Conferences: 1960–1968

I feel it is now high time to turn to the subject, already frequently mentioned, of the training conferences. These meetings were being held in the days before there was a Federation and had rather mothered the Federation – to be adopted, paradoxically, at a later stage by their prosperous and developing child. *The first conference took place in 1960*, when Piet van der Leeuw and H. A. van der Sterren invited representatives of European training bodies to Amsterdam. From the 1964 report it is obvious that the Societies were far from trusting each other with training problems, and still further from co-operating in order to solve them. An attempt to formulate minimal training standards in 1964 failed: the Societies were extremely chary of any international interference. However there was a general feeling that these meetings were important and should continue, and so they did, at two-yearly intervals, in various European cities.

From 1960–1964, Piet van der Leeuw (Amsterdam) was Chairman, and when he became President of the IPA he was succeeded by Wilhelm Solms (Vienna), who organised two, or possibly three more training conferences – certainly, at any rate, the fourth in Paris in 1966 on group supervision and the fifth in Zurich in 1968. From the discussions at these meetings, the differences in training practice in the different Societies became very apparent.

Fritz Morgenthaler conducted an enquiry into the criteria used in each Society in their choice of training analysts, and circulated the data to the various Societies. Later these findings were published in the *Bulletin* of the Swiss Society.

When Wilhelm Solms became President of the EPF, the Council decided that the training conference work should come under the auspices of the Federation, where at that time it was probably more needed and would play a more useful role. In 1971, Adam Limentani (London) succeeded Solms as Convenor of the training conferences, and started to hold them in London.

At this very time the *Bulletin*, 'Psychoanalysis in Europe' came into existence and now the training conferences in their turn could benefit from the Federation since their papers were published in the *Bulletin*. These papers also gave a strong impetus to the *Bulletin*, and it is impressive to see the stimulating effect and the valuable contributions made by the training conferences. From the sixth training conference on, these papers, as long as they were not confidential, were produced in this way. From 1977 onwards, the conference was convened yearly. The papers that appeared in the Bulletin from 1973 onwards have now been issued in a monograph, published in 1983 under the title *Psychoanalytic Training in Europe*.

The significance of these meetings, the problems inherent in them and an attempt at an explanation of their success are best expressed by the following quote from Anne-Marie Sandler (1983):

> these meetings on training antedated the formal founding of the European Federation and have remained a vital aspect of its activities ... Meetings between analysts in Europe have always had to face certain difficulties, not least of them being the need to cross the obvious language and cultural barriers. But there was a further and rather specific difficulty as well. Methods of selection and training differed radically from one group of Societies to another, and different Societies were faced with the task of overcoming their prejudice against 'foreign' methods ... It is remarkable that over the years the [training meetings] have been distinguished by an increasing degree of trust and openness of interchange ... Above all it is due to the absence of a superordinate training body with the power to impose unified methods.

9.   Integration: 1979–1983

When Daniel Widlöcher became President of the Federation (1979) he inherited, metaphorically, a well-designed and well-built house, based on the firm soil of a Constitution that was well adapted to its functions, and kept in good condition by some strong traditions: the Standing Conference on Training, the regular conferences for members on special topics, the Bulletin. These activities provided the individual with ample opportunity for meeting people from other European countries and for discussions on various topics. However the fear arose that conferences alone might become an empty activity; the house had to be furnished as well, and fortunately many opportunities offered themselves. The regular Council Meetings, for instance, created the opportunity and the need for the discussion of specific problems: not all of them spectacular but no less important for that. So one might see this three-and-a-half-year period, from October 1979 to April 1983, as a 'furnishing' period, whereby the large and solid structure that was already there could be used for many smaller activities.

One important factor was the healthy state of the finances.

The capital of the Federation slowly increased and I vividly remember the Treasurer, Alex Pollock, explaining at one Council Meeting that this money was there to be spent, not to be left on deposit in a bank account.

Three suggestions were put forward as to ways of using funds to encourage and support more intimate and personal contacts between European psychoanalysts:

1. for high-level scientific meetings;
2. for meetings with candidates or recently graduated members of the different countries;
3. for visits from senior people to different countries.

Professor Heinz Henseler became chairman of a committee to promote new activities. The other members took part in brainstorming sessions and then Heinz Henseler organised the first *seminar for young associate members at Castle Reisensburg, some distance from Stuttgart, from 3–6 June 1982.* Twenty-seven associate members – not more than two from each Society – and four training analysts from different countries came together. Each training analyst chaired eight clinical seminars so that every associate member could present at least one case, which was thoroughly discussed in groups of seven or eight. All participants agreed that working in this way had been a unique experience.

It is interesting to realise that the idea of such a seminar comes very close to the concept Raymond de Saussure had in mind at the Federation's inception. One of the first tasks, he said, was to arrange some kind of exchange programme for students.

A committee chaired by Janice de Saussure circulated all Societies for information regarding the ways in which they dealt with analysts from another Society who came from abroad to settle in their country. For analysts moving to another country, it was desirable to become a member of the new Society, but what was the attitude of the Societies to foreign analysts?

The aim of this enquiry was rather more to inform analysts intending to move of what they might expect than to tell Societies how to act, apart from the obligation to invite the foreign analysts to scientific meetings. Of course there were certain Societies for whom this presented a serious problem since they were in danger of being flooded by, for example, political refugees from countries with the same mother tongue. It became clear from the findings of this Committee that, apart from the British Society, in most Societies this problem had not been very thoroughly discussed by the membership. The British Society evolved a definite policy for protecting itself, but then Great Britain is very attractive to immigrants. Janice de Saussure wrote (1981):

> Now, with a growing influx of refugees and perhaps an increasing tendency for people to move from one country to another for a variety of reasons, this problem may become more important for all of us. In fact, the autonomy of each Society is really at issue here ... There is also the wider problem of safeguarding the overall well-being of the Society. For example, a relatively small Society might be overwhelmed by an influx of members of other Societies. Or in a new Society admission of even one person with a very different background might cause serious difficulties ...

EPF conferences continued to be held. From 5–8 March 1981, a conference was held in Rome on the theme 'Fantasy and Defence in the Psychoanalytic Process'.

There were 340 participants at the Rome conference. Again the conference was a success, which leads me to Daniel Widlöcher's Presidential Address (1981):

> What is meant by saying that a psychoanalytic congress or conference was a success? ... Everyone agrees that there are too many analytic congresses ... choices must be made ... On what criteria are such choices based? I don't believe

that it is only the theme; I am afraid it is more often considerations of date, of place, and sometimes in connection with a good tour programme!

Widlöcher continues that one quite specific function is to assure members of a feeling of identity. More difficult to appraise is the concept of progress in psychoanalytic knowledge.

Two years later the Fifth Conference of the EPF took place in Jerusalem from 5–8 April 1983. It was attended by 350 people, and the topic, 'The Psychoanalytic Encounter' did indeed consist of clinical presentations where the analysts' own mental processes were recorded as well.

This Jerusalem conference had posed severe problems for the Council, since some of the members of one particular Society had raised objections to holding a conference in a country of whose government's actions they disapproved. After a full discussion in Council, it was decided that the conference should take place in Jerusalem but that Widlöcher, in a Presidential Message, would explain our thoughts on the subject, which he did:

> Since the summer the venue has been arousing a good deal of emotion because of the resumption of war and its consequent atrocities. Opinions have naturally been divergent: some thought that holding a Congress in Jerusalem under these conditions was to lend support to a government whose responsibility in the events was severely criticised, others considered that on the contrary it would show solidarity with the Israeli people ... (1982)

He continues that there are three possible circumstances that would justify cancelling a congress: physical danger to the participants; circumstances where psychoanalysts of the host Society would not be in a position to co-operate with each other, and circumstances where individual freedom and freedom of expression could not be guaranteed. The current situation did not correspond in any way to these three conditions, so the Council decided to keep the conference in Jerusalem.

The standing conferences on training went on annually, convened by Anne-Marie Sandler. And then of course there was the *Bulletin*. Terttu Eskelinen de Folch assumed the office of Editor in 1979. Having stressed the immense difficulties encountered in European psychoanalysis because of the multiplicity of languages, she introduced herself by saying:

> I feel considerable satisfaction as a representative of two small linguistic groups in Europe – Catalan and Finnish – that my election as Editor has brought to the forefront the special difficulties encountered by those who belong to no official linguistic group when participating in the Conferences, since for them communication is hindered by the loss of those subtleties which they have at their command in their mother tongue. (1980)

Mrs Folch organised the offset printing to be done in Barcelona, where it was considerably cheaper than in London. A publishing committee was formed in Barcelona, headed by Dr Salvador Adroer and assisted, in the ever-growing volume of work, by his whole family, Mrs Gloria Estruch, Dr Joan Estruch and his wife, Heide Axmacher.

10.   1985 to the Present

Anne-Marie Sandler, the new President, arranged an extraordinary Council Meeting to take place at the IPA congress in Madrid in order to plan for the immediate future. It had already been decided that the seminars for associate members should be continued. The second seminar was to take place in the Priory of Corsendonk in Belgium; again two delegates were invited from each Society and the seminar was supervised by four experienced training analysts from different countries. It became apparent at this second seminar that the requirement that associate members present a case in two of the three official languages of the Federation had become an insoluble problem, especially for small Societies in countries where none of the official languages was spoken. It seemed that either the bilingual requirement, or the stipulation that different individuals be sent each time, might have to be dropped. Nevertheless all the participants were extremely appreciative of their encounter with different techniques and greatly fascinated by the experience of being able to present material freely without being judged. The organisers of the third seminar, at King's College, Cambridge in 1985 – L. Sohn and S. Davies – solved the language problem in another way: by making English the sole language.

In one of the first Council Meetings with Daniel Widlöcher, the idea was put forward of organising an event to serve not only neglected areas of the membership (the seminars for associate members) but neglected topics as well. In this way the symposia on controversial concepts were conceived, of which two were organised: one in Marseilles in 1984 on 'The Death Drive', the other in Divonne-les-Bains on 'Drives and Affects' in 1986. The aim of these symposia is to offer the opportunity for high-level discussion on specific concepts, thereby promoting European scientific exchange.

The symposium on 'The Death Drive' has been reported on in detail by Pere Folch and Terttu Eskelinen de Folch (1984). Introductory papers were given by J.-B. Laplanche, Hanna Segal, André Green and Eero Rechardt, and will be issued as a monograph. The extensive discussion gave rise to much controversy, which finally came down, oddly enough, not to any controversy about the concept but about the way to interpret it.

The symposium in Divonne-les-Bains was organised in the same way, although it was decided that three papers would suffice. René Diatkine, Leon Grinberg and Joseph Sandler presented their views on the theme 'Drives and Affects'. The discussion, as in Marseilles, was extremely lively on the controversial aspects of the views of presenters and discussants.

The languages spoken at these symposia were French and English and there were enough participants speaking both languages well to provide ad hoc translations. It was clear that these symposia were very desirable in bridging the gap between scientists in different European countries.

In one of the discussions, Eugenic Gaddini suggested a larger training conference, open to all training analysts instead of two delegates. This suggestion was realised for the first time in Paris in June 1984.

Every two years a Council Meeting is devoted to some special topic, as initiated in Amsterdam in 1982, in the meeting on 'Psychoanalysis and the State'. In 1984 the Council met in Geneva to discuss 'Psychoanalysis and the University' and in 1986 in Windsor to discuss the problem of the teaching of psychotherapy by psychoanalysts.

Whether the Federation actually has the right to celebrate its twentieth birthday now (1986) is highly debatable. Although the Executive Council of the Federation, together with the Presidents of the officially recognised Societies, voted for the Federation on 2 October 1966, it was not officially recognised by the IPA until 28 July 1969, in Rome. It might be appropriate to have a second celebration of the Federation's twentieth anniversary at the 1989 Congress in that same Rome, twenty years on.

11. Conclusions

Anybody who has read the earlier sections will have discovered that I have limited myself to a description of those persons and events contributing to a climate in which psychoanalysis can be studied and practised. I have hardly spoken about psychoanalysis itself. Although it would be interesting to find out whether and how the climate and practice of psychoanalysis influence each other, this would require many years of research?

But what is the use, one might now ask, of all this fact gathering?

I would like to point out how the facts prove again, firstly that psychoanalysis is a potent symbol of mental freedom, and secondly that freedom of opinion and free discussion in Societies are fundamental to psychoanalytic practice. The first point is illustrated by the way in which psychoanalysis in France and Holland prospered underground during the German occupation and by the way in which August Aichhorn in Austria and Imre Hermann in Hungary managed to sow the seeds in preparation for a rebirth when the time was ripe. The second point is shown in the very short time that elapsed between the establishment of democracy and the foundation of study groups, or of the recognition of Societies in Belgium after the German occupation, in Madrid after Franco's death, in Portugal after the establishment of democracy and in Greece after the disappearance of the Colonels' regime. Conversely we lost our little Czechoslovakian group and saw the disappearance of Polish psychoanalysis when political developments severely restricted freedom of opinion. We should keep such factors in mind when we are too ready to embrace governments because they want to subsidise psychoanalysis. Financial dependence on a third party might prove in the end to be almost as restrictive of mental freedom as totalitarian suppression is.

12. Movements

One aspect of European history has endured: every Society in every country still has its own cultural and linguistic background, and each separate country has been at war with every other separate country at some time in the last few hundred years. A basic sense that 'we are different' and a mild basic mistrust will probably persist in Europe forever. A contrary affective impulse, which is apparently stronger than the dividing one, is the fact that psychoanalysts need each other. Green (1976) asks: 'How can one remain a psychoanalyst?' (p. 19) in his analysis of 'The Privacy of the Self' by Masud Khan (1974). His answer is:

> The only solution lies in friendship. It is often said that an analyst's best friends are often analysts. The profession which they share is not the only reason.

Green goes on to say that in the relationship that analysts have with one another they can find:

> friendship which our practice forbids us to have with our patients ... In this, finally, lies an additional ground of praise for that agreed distance which wishes to share affection, yet is anxious to respect the other.' (p. 20)

In this last paragraph I have tried to offer arguments to substantiate my hypothesis that the ups and downs of the European Federation through the twenty or so years of its existence are only partly due to the direct action or, in some instances, to the inaction of individuals. It is of course self-evident that men with vision and a willingness to work hard in order to reach a well-defined goal are absolutely essential for founding and structuring the Federation. However there are other factors which put a limit on what can be done to bridge the gaps of inertia and depression. These factors are partly inherent in the peculiarities of our own individualistic European Society with its many valuable and sometimes troublesome traditions based upon cultural and linguistic differences. Other factors are inherent in the impossible profession of being an analyst and its influence on those who practise this profession.

References

ANZIEU, A. (1972). The Anglo-French Colloquium, Broadway, 1972. *EPF Bull. 1*, 10–12.

BAKER, R., LETARTE, P., & HOMMES, M. (1977). Technical problems of interpretation: report. *EPF Bull. 11*, 8–13.

DE BLÉCOURT, A. (1973). Similarities and differences between training analysis and therapeutic analysis. *EPF Bull. 2*.

BRECHT, K., FRIEDRICH, V., HERMANNS, L. M., KAMINER, I. J., & JULIEN, D. H. (1985). *'Hier geht das Leben auf eine sehr merkwürdige Weise weiter ...' Zur Geschichte der Psychoanalyse in Deutschland*. Hamburg: Michael Kellner.

BUSINESS MEETING OF THE IPA IN ROME, 1969 (1970). Bull, of the IPA. *Int. J. Psycho-Anal. 51*, 95–113.

BUSINESS MEETING: COMPREHENSIVE SUMMARY OF PROCEEDINGS (1976). 14'st Bull, of the IPA. *Int. J. Psycho-Anal. 57*, 187.

EJVE, B. (1984). On the activities of the Swedish Society. *EPF Bull. 22*, 105–110.

ESKELINEN DE FOLCH, T. (1980). Editorial. *EPF Bull. 15*, 2–3.

ESKELINEN DE FOLCH, T. (1985). Note from the Editor. *EPF Bull. 24*, 3–4.

ESKELINEN DE FOLCH, T., DELAHAYE, B., GODFRIND, J., WATILLON, A., JENSEN, R., & CARELS, N, (1984). Reports on the Second European Psychoanalytic Seminar. *EPF Bull. 22*, 79–86.

EUROPEAN PSYCHOANALYTICAL FEDERATION (1972). 137th Bulletin of the IPA. *Int. J.Psycho-Anal. 53*, 117.

EUROPEAN PSYCHOANALYTICAL FEDERATION (1980). 144th Bulletin of the IPA. *Int. J. Psycho-Anal. 61*, 118–120.

FIRST CONFERENCE OF THE EPF (1978). 143rd Bulletin of the IPA. *Int. J. Psycho-Anal. 59*, 101–102.

FOLCH, P., & ESKELINEN DE FOLCH, T. (1984). Report on the EPF symposium on the death drive. *EPF Bull. 22*, 51–78.

FREUD, S. (1914). On the history of the psycho-analytic movement. *S.E, 14*.

GREEN, A. (1976). The other and the experience of the Self. *BPP Bull. 7*, 7–20.

GROEN-PRAKKEN, H. (1981). Psychoanalysis in the Netherlands: victim of economic recession? *EPF Bull. 17*, 99–100.

GROEN-PRAKKEN, H. (1984). Report from the Dutch Society. *EPP Bull. 22*, 111–114.

HAVNEGJERDE, H., & HELMERS, E. (1977). The Norwegian Psychoanalytical Society. *EPF Bull. 12*, 14–15.

HENSELER, H. (1982). Report on the first European Psychoanalytic Seminar. *EPF Bull. 19*, 61–62.

HERMANN, I., & PETO, E. (1946). Hungarian Psychoanalytical Society. Bull, of the IPA. *Int. J. Psycho-Anal. 27*, 87–92.

HERTZ, D. (1982). Fifty years of psychoanalysis in Israel: a report on the Israel Psychoanalytic Society. *EPF Bull. 19*, 79–86.

HILDEBRAND, H. P. (1972). Editorial. *EPF Bull. 1*, 1–2.

HOLDER, A. (1976). Summary of the meeting between the Council of the EPF and the Presidents of European Societies. *EPF Bull. 8*, 1–2.

HOLDER, A. (1981). Report on the 4th Conference of the Federation, Rome, 5–8 March 1981. *EPF Bull. 16*, 77–82.

JONES, E. (1939). Opening Address: Bulletin of the IPA. *Int. J. Psycho-Anal. 20*, 116.

KESTENBERG, J. (1971). Contributions de la psychanalyse des enfants (Symposium, Geneva 1970). *Psychiatr. Enfant 14*, 5–6.

KING, P. (1983). The life and work of Melanie Klein in the British Society. *Int. J. Psycho-Anal. 64*, 251–260.

LAGACHE, D. (1945). Report on the psychoanalytical activities of the Institute of Psychology of the University of Strasbourg, moved to Clermont-Ferrand, from November 1940–December 1944. Bull, of the IPA. *Int. J. Psycho-Anal. 26*, 85–86.

LAPLANCHE, J., & PONTALIS, J.-B. (1967). *The Language of Psychoanalysis*. London: Hogarth Press, 1973.

LEBOVICI, S. (1986). Some recollections of the foundation of the European federation of psychoanalytic Societies. *EPF Bull. 26–27*, 73–78.

VAN DER LEEUW, P.J. (1947). Report. *Int. J. Psycho-Anal. 28*, 214–219.

VAN DER LEEUW, P.J. (1965). Studi sulla unificazione dei metodi di insegnamento della psicoanalisi in seno ai Comitati Europei di Training (with an introduction by I. Tolentino). *Estratto della Rivista di Psiaoanalisi, 11*, 194–203.

VAN DER LEEUW, P.J. (1970). Four years' presidency: a personal view. *Int. J. Psycho-Anal. 51*, 49.

VAN DER LEEUW, P.J. (1985). Personal communications: an interview. Unpublished.

LEUBA, J. (1945). Activities of the French Psychoanalytical Society during the German occupation. Bull, of the IPA. *Int. J. Psycho-Anal. 26*, 84–85.

LEUPOLD-LÖWENTHAL, H. (1982). Verfolgung und Krieg in der Geschichte der Psychoanalyse in Wien. In H. HENSELER & A. KUCHENBUCH (Eds.), *Die Wiederkehr von Krieg und Verfolgung in Psychoanalyse* (Privately printed).

LIMENTANI, A. (1986). Variations on Freudian themes. *Int. J. Psycho-Anal. 67*, 235–243.

LOEWENSTEIN, R.M. (1973). Raymond de Saussure 1894–1971. *Int. J. Psycho-Anal. 53*, 111–112.

MEKKING, R.U. (1972). Psychoanalysis in Europe. *EPF Bull. 1*, 2–5.

MEKKING, R.U. (1976). Training in psychotherapy ... within or outside the psychoanalytical Societies. *EPF Bull. 8*, 2–6.

MINUTES OF THE MEETING OF THE GENERAL ASSEMBLY OF THE EPF, held on Thursday, 25 August 1977, at the Convention Centre Jerusalem (1977). *EPF Bull. 12*, 1–4.

DE M'UZAN, M. (1976). The economics of mental functioning in relation to psychosomatic disturbance. *EPF Bull. 8*, 6–10.

NEMES, L. (1985). Das Schicksal der ungarischen Psychoanalytiker in den Jahren des Faschismus. In K. BRECHT et al. (Eds.). *Hier geht das Leben auf eine sehr merkwürdige Weise weiter ...* Hamburg: Michael Kellner, pp. 82–85.

NEYRAUT-SUTTERMAN, TH. (1972). The first candidates' pre-congress in Europe. *EPF Bull. 1*, 7–10.

POKORNY, M. (1972). European Candidates' Federation. *EPF Bull. 1*, 6–7.

SANDLER, A.-M. (1983). *Introduction to Psychoanalytic Training in Europe*. EPF Monograph.

SANDLER, J. (1976). Letter from the President of the European Psychoanalytical Federation. *EPF Bull. 7*, 1–2.

SANDLER, J. (1978). Message from the President. *EPF Bull. 13*, 3.

SANDLER, J. (1980). The negative therapeutic reaction: an introduction. *EPF Bull. 15*, 13–18.

SANDLER, J. (1982). Anna Freud: an obituary. *EPF Bull. 19*, 11.

DE SAUSSURE, J. (1981). Report on the attitudes of Societies to reciprocal membership arrangements. *EPF Bull. 17*, 101–104.

DE SAUSSURE, R. (1969). Editorial in Bulletin d'Information de la Federation Européenne Psychanalytique.

DE SAUSSURE, R., & SOLMS, W. (1968). Report on the training regulations of European Societies. *Bull. Swiss Society 8*, 68–69.

SERVADIO, E. (1981). The Italian Psychoanalytical Society. *EPF Bull. 16*, 71–72.

SOLMS, W. (1972). From the President of the EPF. *EPF Bull. 1*, 5–6.

SOLMS, W. (1975). In Memoriam. *EPF Bull. 6*, 29.

VAN DER STERREN, H. A. (1946). Dutch Psychoanalytical Society: Report. Bull, of the IPA. *Int. J. Psycho-Anal. 27*, 83–86.

SUMMARY OF IMPORTANT ACTIVITIES WITHIN THE ASSOCIATION (1970). 133rd Bull, of the IPA. *Int. J. Psycho-Anal. 51*, 113–131.

TAMM, A. (1945). Swedish Society. Bull, of the IPA. *Int. J. Psycho-Anal. 26*, 86–87.

WIDLÖCHER, D. (1973). On communication within the psychoanalytic community. *EPF Bull. 3*, 1–5.

WIDLÖCHER, D. (1977). The professional career of the psychoanalyst and problems of training. *EPF Bull. 11*, 2–6.

WIDLÖCHER, D. (1978). Editor's Introduction. *EPF Bull. 13*, 2.

WIDLÖCHER, D. (1981). The Congress was a success … *EPF Bull. 17*, 7–9.

WIDLÖCHER, D. (1982). Message from the President. *EPF Bull. 19*, 7–10.

'The Congress was a Success …'

Daniel Widlöcher
(with additional remarks by Leopoldo Bleger)

Owing to the impossibility of writing a piece for our book, we are publishing be-
low, with his permission, a piece that Daniel Widlöcher read during the 1981
EPF congress. Despite its date, it seems to us entirely topical.

At the presentation of the EPF Award for a Distinguished Contribution
to Psychoanalysis on 14th June 2015, Daniel Widlöcher said a few words that
seemed to us to embody the entirety of his strength, in particular his question
concerning the 'pleasure of thinking':

> *One is not a psychoanalyst by oneself. We do not share everything, but we can count*
> *on a kind of extremely important collegial friendship, a tie between friends and*
> *colleagues, with our predecessors and masters. We belong to a community in which*
> *we abide together.*
>
> *The pleasure of being an analyst is a shared dimension. In a way, it is a matter*
> *of enjoyment in thought. We share something in common, we are familiar with its*
> *dangers and risks.*
>
> *In a certain way, psychoanalysis represents a pleasure in thinking. This is a*
> *point that some might find scandalous. How may one be pleased with psychoanaly-*
> *sis and in one's capacity as an analyst? There is an erroneous point of thought that*
> *spurs to sing the praises of psychoanalysis. Such an affirmation might irritate, in-*
> *deed, disturb. However, it is not a matter of singing the praises of psychoanalysis*
> *but rather of acknowledging a certain pleasure tied to its practice. For behind it*
> *all is the question: Why do we have the pleasure, in a certain way, in thinking*
> *together?*

The congress was a success ...[1]

What is meant by saying that a psychoanalytic congress or conference was a success? I am not speaking here of material success although that is no small part, considering the effort required for the organisation of a congress. It is indeed one necessary condition but not enough. It is also interesting to ask ourselves by what scientific criteria we judge psychoanalysts' communications among themselves.

Everyone agrees that there are too many analytic congresses. For each one, choices must be made and the expenses involved in participating at international reunions are such that these choices can only be very limited in any one year. On what criteria are such choices based? I don't believe that it is only the theme; I am afraid it is more often considerations of date, of place, and sometimes in connection with a good tour programme! Besides, it seems to me that 'senior' analysts are less and less active and that many travel only when they are involved in an administrative capacity or are actively participating in a scientific programme. The less 'senior' are, in this respect, more indulgent and doubtless find more of interest in the scientific reunions, whether because they are impressed by the academic aspect of the reunion, or on account of a personal curiosity with regard to the speaker. It wouldn't be a bad idea to go into this more thoroughly and consider the function of scientific communication in psychoanalysis.

In the first place, we must take into account one very specific function of psychoanalytic communications: that is, to assure members of a feeling of identity. This is not merely a matter of so-called narcissistic reinforcement, but we know that psychoanalysis is always a poorly defined undertaking, which each one must determine in his own practice. All the definitions that have been given are determined by a combination of a set of rules for technique (the psychoanalytic setting) and the theoretical foundations that help us to understand the material. These are two complementary elements that demand a continual adjustment from us. It is natural that many variations are practised and we must continually examine the effects of technique on theory and of theory on technique. By studying thoroughly the differences that exist in these two areas, we are better able to grasp what is common to us all. Of

---

1   Originally published in the EPF *Bulletin*, 17, pp. 7–10.

course, these variations must not appear to be excessively divergent, otherwise we run the risk of no longer meeting each other. In adapting our own understanding to original contributions or in opposing them, we are developing our own identities.

What is more difficult to appraise is the concept of progress in psychoanalytic knowledge. It is highly embarrassing when a stranger to psychoanalysis asks what was new in the scientific contributions of a congress. And our difficulty in replying to such a question often plunges the enquirer into a perplexity frequently bordering on scepticism. I think it would be particularly interesting for us to consider this notion of scientific progress in psychoanalysis. If we look back retrospectively to different congresses and reunions in which we have participated during the past few years, how can we define progress?

The first field for conjecture is the progress of knowledge in the area of pathology. This is a subject that has already been widely explored. The expansion of indications for psychoanalysis to different pathological organisations (psychosis, borderline states, narcissism, psychosomatics, perversion ...) has had some not inconsiderable effects on our practice and theory. Without any doubt, the experience of psychoanalysts in these different areas has made a contribution of the first importance in the psychopathology of clinical states. But psychoanalysts are more interested in the results of all this on the understanding of the psychoanalytic process than in the progress of psychiatric nosology. There is often a feeling that attention to a particular psychopathological structure is a new grid that we apply to our everyday work. Isn't sensitivity to the narcissistic dimension or to the process of individuation very often a new way of listening to the patient and of understanding his mental life? At times, one even has the feeling that this drift leads to a reformulation of means and ends in psychoanalysis. Indeed is it a matter of progress or of a drift? Of a progress in knowledge, of an evolution, or of a technical and theoretical drift?

In the area of so-called theory, meetings are less lively in Europe than elsewhere. Rare are the discussions devoted to a revision of metapsychology, to the theory of the self, or to that of drives. Yet there would be a great deal to say on the differences and divergences in this area. What is more discernible among European analysts is the interest shown in the use we can make of theories and methods foreign to psychoanalysis, but capable of livening its concepts (linguistics, social sciences, biology).

It is in the area of technique that the idea of progress emerges least clearly. We seem to find great resistance in approaching such a subject openly, as if it were a question of an intangible element or as if all discussions on varying techniques relate rather to a theory of psychotherapy than of psychoanalysis proper. However, on closer examination, it is perhaps precisely here that the evolution of psychoanalytic thought is most palpable: no doubt less apropos technique proper than the knowledge of mental processes that are observed in the patient and in the analyst. Our knowledge of transference and countertransference, and the use we make of them in treatment, has changed considerably during the course of the last two decades and it's time to evaluate this evolution and to discuss the developments. It could be a particularly useful task for European psychoanalysts, insofar as we could surely observe perceptible differences amongst ourselves, but also see some originality of approach vis-à-vis our colleagues over the Atlantic.

Scientific communication and progress in knowledge are not the only themes dealt with. We could just as well take up the way in which meetings are conducted. Everyone agrees in considering that reference to clinical material is an irreplaceable method. But in fact, we find great embarrassment when it comes to talking about a case. Recourse to short 'vignettes' is not always the best solution. Material summarised and stripped of its context scarcely serves to illustrate a theoretical concept and lends little to the discussion, Nor is the presentation of a case in more detail without disadvantages. Too often, this leads to a sort of collective supervision in which everyone tries his psychoanalytic talents on the material of others. It seems to me that the best clinical presentations are those which report in detail a session or a fragment of a session, especially if the author can also take into account his own mental processes. This method is the most revealing as far as the patient and indeed the analyst himself is concerned. I have the impression that analysts have much more to learn in working skilfully with such material. Perhaps congresses are not the best place for perfecting this mode of exchange and reunions of smaller groups would make for greater progress.

One other aspect of the meeting always surprises me: the difficulty of setting up a real discussion with opposing views. Glover's remark is worth noting, in this respect:

> Analysts of established prestige and seniority produce papers advancing a new theoretical or clinical viewpoint or discovery. If others corroborate it they tend

to report that; but if others feel reason to reject it, this scientific 'negative' does not get reported. So, ultimately it is canonized 'as so-and-so has shown'.

The interventions following a report are more often monologues than discussions. These are no doubt feared because of the narcissistic wounds that are anticipated. Here again, one can imagine progress in psychoanalytic communication with the establishment of real discussions, possibly carried on from one meeting to another, without fearing that differences or even conflicting standpoints, will threaten this feeling of identity of which we have such a need.

Anne-Marie Sandler and the EPF

An interview with Eva Schmid-Gloor, 29 August 2015

Anne-Marie Sandler has been linked to and engaged in the EPF since its very first beginning.

In an interview with Eva Schmid-Gloor, she talks about her memories of the start of the EPF and the different stages of her involvement.

At the very start of the EPF, Anne-Marie Sandler remembers:
'I experienced the start of the EPF somehow "second hand", through the engagement of my husband Joe, who was very taken by the idea of founding a European Psychoanalytic Community. He had met Raymond de Saussure from Geneva (Switzerland), who had come back from the USA with many years of experience of North American psychoanalysis. Raymond de Saussure was different from the usual psychoanalyst, because he had travelled a lot, not only in the States, but also all over Europe and had friendly links with many colleagues internationally. He was the first to envisage the creation of a European Association that would include all European Societies. He was convinced that such an association would greatly enrich the varied but rather isolated European Societies.

Joe was at the time very much aware of the richness of the British Society, but also of its isolation. British analysts were considering very novel and interesting issues, markedly different from the classical teaching of Freud. When the Freud family came to London as refugees after Hitler's invasion of Austria, the conflicts between the classical Freudian ideas and the Kleinian ones emerged and both sides were forced to reflect more profoundly and become clearer about the different points of views they represented.

Joe and I, through this experience, realized the richness of being forced to face different theoretical understandings and clinical approaches in our various psychoanalytic Societies. So when Raymond came up with the idea of creating a European Society, making exchanges with as many European Societies as possible, Joe agreed to support Raymond de Saussure as much as he could.

Raymond, together with representatives from England, Finland, Italy, Germany and Austria, as far as I can remember, soon made a solid and keen group. It was clear from the beginning that a European Association would have to be something totally different from the IPA. It should concentrate on pure scientific meetings of the different European traditions and in no way interfere or control trainings or politics of individual Societies.

The idea of a European Federation was gradually met with enthusiasm in England as well as in Holland, Belgium, Germany and also in the Scandinavian countries and in Italy. However, it was clear from the beginning that the French were very cautious. I think that they were quite anxious that a European psychoanalytic community would slowly become a second IPA. Raymond de Saussure had close links with both the French Societies and tried to persuade them that this was not the case. Progress was very slow, but finally both French Societies accepted the idea.

The very first European Conference took place in Geneva in June 1970 and was mostly organised by Raymond de Saussure. It was a symposium on child analysis with the overall title of 'The Role of the Analysis of Children in the Education of the Analyst'. René Diatkine from Paris, and Anna Freud and Hanna Segal from London were the three invited speakers. René Diatkine's paper was entitled 'Preliminary Comments on the Actual State of Child Analysis'. Anna Freud spoke of 'Child Analysis as a Sub-Speciality of Psychoanalysis and Hanna Segal presented her ideas on 'The Role of Child Analysis in the Analytic Training'. The discussions were very animated and I remember that all the Societies that by now had become part of the European Federation were well represented.'

Eva Schmid-Gloor: 'How did you personally experience the first exchanges at the level of European meetings?'

Anne-Marie Sandler: 'I found the exchanges stimulating and refreshing, as they tended to address different and fresh aspects of psychoanalytical theory or practice. When Joe became President of the EPF we had a second conference in Aix-en-Provence with a variety of papers. At that early period of the European Federation we were not yet a very large group and we were poor. So there was no question of employing translators. The people who were bilingual among the 40 or 45 participants were asked to help. Which we did in a very painstaking way: the presenter read half a page and stopped. His text was translated in one corner from English into German or from German into English and in another corner from English to French or from French to English. The presenter then read the second half of his first page and so it went on. Surprisingly, it worked, because everybody had this enthusiasm for this kind of togetherness and participated in the effort to understand each other. It was a wonderful conference.

Eva Schmid-Gloor: 'What a start! How do you remember the development of the structures of the EPF?'

Anne-Marie Sandler: 'The European Federation was first organised along the classical way with a Committee, a President, one or two Vice Presidents etc., very much like most Societies or like the IPA. When Joe took over, he decided that the by-laws would have to be changed completely. One great innovation was that he installed a Council, composed of the presidents of each Society at the centre of the organisation. The presidents of each European Society who joined the EPF became, together with the European Federation-elected President, the two Vice-Presidents, the General Secretary, the Treasurer, and an Editor of the *Bulletin*, responsible for the activities and decisions of the EPF. At the time we were around 15 or 16 Societies. When the French – who had at first been so hesitant and sceptical – joined us, we finally succeeded in creating discussions about our different ideas about training in an open and free way. We could learn so much from the differences.'

Eva Schmid-Gloor: 'I think this process is still going on. The discussions inside the Forum on Education are surely still having an impact on both sides also nowadays.'

Anne-Marie Sandler: 'For sure! The Forum was in our times called the Standing Conference on Education and the discussions around the differences in admission-procedures, supervision, evaluation etc. were always very rich and precious.

Very soon Joe organised also the so-called New Member Seminar to bring young analysts together on a European level. At the time we paid for the students to attend these meetings. Each Society could send two people.

The next initiative was to organise every second year a small symposium for experienced analysts. We had one on the Death Instinct and another on 'What is the ego?' I don't remember that it continued, which is a pity.'

Eva Schmid-Gloor: 'Perhaps we restarted it in some way, by introducing an EPF Symposium 2014 in Berlin. Another question: Do you remember titles of conferences in your times and what do you think of the development of EPF Conference titles?'

Anne-Marie Sandler: 'It's difficult to remember in detail. We can read it in the *Bulletin*. But I do think, specially with Serge [Frisch], there has been an opening-up and originality in the titles of conferences, which I find very, very refreshing. It's new and wonderful, instead of the same slightly boring way of looking at defences, conflicts etc. The titles have become much more varied, open and intriguing in the last few years.'

Eva Schmid-Gloor: 'What do you remember from the beginnings of the EPF, concerning the link between EPF and IPA?'

Anne-Marie Sandler: 'I don't remember any conflicts at all. Crucially, our aims were different. I never had any dealings with the IPA during my presidency and, as far as I remember, it was the same before and after my time as President of the EPF.'

Eva Schmid-Gloor: 'These days, European Representatives of the IPA Board are always present in a part of our Council Meeting. How was it in your times?'

Anne-Marie Sandler: 'I am wondering who decided this. It may have started during the presidency of David Tuckett who contacted the IPA to get financial support for the various working parties that he had introduced in the

EPF. This may have been the start of the present situation. As I do not believe that the EPF receives any funds from the IPA any longer, it seems that the presence of representatives of the IPA during your business meetings is an anomaly.'

Eva Schmid-Gloor: 'Thank you for this comment. Could you now let me know some spontaneous memories of the times of your own presidency of the EPF?'

Anne-Marie Sandler: 'I took over from Daniel Widlöcher as the fifth President of EPF in Jerusalem and was in charge of the EPF from 1983 to 1987. I found an institution that was working well and I felt that what was important was to continue to facilitate an increased exchange of clinical and theoretical work between Societies at the conferences, which at that time took place every second year. I don't think that during my four years at the helm I introduced much novelty. I felt, it was time to let our members get used to our European encounters and exchanges. Hanna Segal, André Green and Joe Sandler were very active in participating in our various conferences and all our meetings were very well attended ... From the beginning of being an analyst you have to find sufficient solidity to know where you stand as an analyst, but at the same time you have to have a kind of freedom that allows you to accept that there is not one psychoanalysis, but many. So what is it that these other people do so successfully? Is it simply that they have different patients, or that some patients need different methods? Thanks to the EPF I gained a greater awareness of the fact that other people work differently and it doesn't disturb me any more. Others are not bad or stupid, they are thinking differently and probably their environment is different – The EPF helped me a lot into realising this fact.'

Eva Schmid-Gloor: 'Dear Anne-Marie, thank you so much for sharing these thoughts with us!'

The EPF in the 1990s: Expansion and Creativity

Alain Gibeault

Founded in 1967 at the instigation of Raymond de Saussure, the European Psychoanalytical Federation became, thirty years later at the end of the 1990s, an influential organisation through its efforts at developing scientific exchanges across the European psychoanalytic Societies and at overcoming difficulties related to cultural, linguistic and institutional differences. At the time the EPF brought together around 3,700 members from 19 countries speaking 16 different languages. It was made up of 21 Societies and three Study Groups (the Czech group, the Belgrade group and the Polish group).

The European Psychoanalytical Federation has always viewed its role as a locus of exchange and a forum for ideas for the psychoanalytic Societies in Europe. From this point of view, its vocation has always been essentially *scientific*, contrary to that of the International Psychoanalytical Association, whose function is likewise *political* in so far as it is the guarantor of the 'shared tenets' uniting all psychoanalysts who are its members. If the EPF discusses problems concerning training, the IPA presents itself as a body guaranteeing training and psychoanalytic policy according to a minimum set of standards.

This distinction, in principal clear, was nevertheless challenged by the tendency within psychoanalytic Societies to restructure the IPA in order to take into account the demographic increase of its members and the necessity of finding more adequate representation for the Societies themselves. In effect, if the European Federation is foremost a federation of Societies whose presidents constitute the EPF Council together with the Executive, the International Psychoanalytical Association is foremost an association of individual members, which the structure moreover of its Council attests to, constituted at the time by individually elected members. As the 1990s drew to a close, we were obliged to consider the European Federation's destiny in relation to important changes within the IPA and in the life of the psychoanalytic Societies.

This is the venture, the source of both conflicts and innovation, which I would like to touch on here. I was a member of the EPF Executive Committee during the years comprising my term of office as President, from 1995 to 1999. Betty Denzler assisted me very efficiently as General Secretary during these four years, which laid the ground for the considerable changes in our international institutions throughout the course of the turn of the century.[1]

I.   The scientific life of the EPF

At its beginnings, the EPF restricted itself in practice to the organisation of an annual conference on training, and the publication – beginning in 1972 – of an annual, twenty-page *Bulletin*. Nearly 30 years later, the EPF was organising more than ten various scientific encounters and publishing a 120 page, biannual *Bulletin*.

The organisation of a *Standing Conference on Training*, which took place each autumn in London, went hand in hand with the EPF's evolution since its founding. After more than 20 years of continuous discussion on training, it seemed necessary in the 1990s to modify the rhythm of these meetings and breathe some fresh air into them in order to get past their somewhat repetitive character; hence the idea of organising a standing conference on training in a city different from London and dissociating it from when the English-language conference would take place. This is why the EPF Council decided, in the autumn of 1994, to organise these two meetings on training

---

1   I further wish to point out the friendly and constant work of the other members of the Executive Committee during the course of these four years. For 1995–1997: James Innes-Smith and Henk Jan Dalewijk (Vice Presidents); Alex Pollock (Treasurer); and Gabriele Junkers (Bulletin Editor). For 1997–1999: James Innes-Smith (President Elect); Emma Piccioli and Imre Szecsödy (Vice Presidents); Henk Jan Dalewijk (Treasurer); and Gabriele Junkers (Bulletin Editor). We were also confronted by the sudden death of James Innes-Smith during the course of his term as President Elect.

in rotation as well as to modify their names: a *Colloquium on Training*, still implicating two delegates per Society, generally engaged in the organisation of the Commissions on Teaching; and a *Conference for Training Analysts* open to all European training analysts, which took place in the autumn of 1998 in Athens on the theme of analytic training models.

For a long time it seemed vital not to separate child and adolescent analysis from adult analysis. Certain European congresses regularly included clinical cases beginning with infancy through adulthood and went into problems on the setting and analytic technique according to the different life stages. However, the diversity of approaches and problems concerning practice and training led the EPF to separate the scientific meetings on adult psychoanalysis and child and adolescent psychoanalysis.

At first these conferences were intended for two delegates per Society who were primarily committed to training and the practice of child and adolescent analysis. As for the conferences on training, the necessity of opening scientific meetings up to all analysts led to the organisation of a broader conference, which took place in London in November 1994 on the theme of 'The Formulation of Transference Interpretations Today'. Thus began the alternating of a *Colloquium on Child and Adolescent Psychoanalysis*, open to two delegates per Society, and a *Conference on Child and Adolescent Psychoanalysis*, open to all European analysts.

The process leading to differentiating training and technique intensified. The founding in the 1990s of the European Association for Adolescent Psychoanalysis (EAAP) by Moses Laufer and other European colleagues had already aimed at encouraging research on adolescent analysis; the EPF Council favourably welcomed the possible project of dissolving this association and taking up its objectives within an EPF commission on adolescent psychoanalysis.

Encouraged by this significant research trend, the EPF organised a *Colloquium on Child and Adolescent Psychoanalysis* in 1997 in Milan on the theme of 'Similarities and Differences between Child and Adolescent Psychoanalysis' with Florence Guignard, Moses Laufer and Antonino Ferro participating. It was a matter of reviving the theme that had given rise to previous EPF meetings on these fields and possibly envisaging the need to organise separate scientific encounters on child analysis and adolescent analysis so as to respect their technical and clinical differences. As for the meetings on training, these research projects thus contributed to increasing scientific encounters, with the risk of a decrease in the number of participants.

The *Associate Members Seminar* would go through the same success, due to the unique opportunity offered to every young colleague of presenting a clinical case to a small group of analysts coming from all European countries and of sharing in the experience of different training analysts. Moreover, the initiative taken in 1984 to organise a *Scientific Symposium* every two years continued during the 1990s. The objective of these encounters was to make possible the conditions for high-level scientific discussions on controversial psychoanalytic concepts, which in particular brought out the differences and likenesses between the French and British approaches. Among the themes gone into at the time were: 'What is an Object?' (Vienna, 1990); 'Transformations of the Object in the Transference' (Helsinki, 1992); 'The Different Levels of Interpretation' (Limelette, 1996); and 'Psychoanalysts Speak to Psychoanalysts: Communication in the Psychoanalytic Community Today' (Jerusalem, 1998).

Lastly, every two years the EPF organised a large *congress* open to all members and candidates from the European psychoanalytic Societies. This congress grew rapidly, in particular thanks to simultaneous translation of the three official languages of the EPF. Organised by different European Societies, it first took place in Geneva in March 1997 on the theme of 'Borderline States and Hysteria' and brought together approximately 450 participants. It was at this congress that André Green introduced his concept of the *chiasmus* between hysteria and borderline states.

The next congress took place for the first time in Berlin, in March 1999, and made possible a discussion of a subject that clearly expressed the challenges of Europe and European psychoanalysis at the dawn of the 21st century: 'Love, Hate and Violence: a Contemporary Challenge for Psychoanalysis' – a subject that referred as much to the individual construction of the psyche as to collective life, as the history of Europe with its conflicts and divisions had shown, but also its promises of union beyond splitting. From this perspective, no city but Berlin, which became the capital of Germany in 1999, could better symbolise the desire for union between individuals and peoples beyond the East-West divide. This is true for collective history but also for that of psychoanalysis: already in Freud's time, Berlin was an influential centre of psychoanalytic life when the first psychoanalytic institute was founded and, through its geographic position at the heart of Europe and its historic tradition, it was destined to play an essential role in the opening up of Eastern Europe and the exchanges between European psychoanalytic Societies. This is what the EPF wished to emphasise when it accepted the invitation of the German Association to organise the 1999 congress in Berlin.

From 1990 onwards, Europeans and North Americans met every two years for a clinical exchange on the model of the Associate Members Seminar: small discussion groups worked simultaneously as each participant was invited to present during an hour and a half meeting a clinical case focusing on a few sessions. The number of participants was restricted to around forty Europeans and an equal number of North Americans. These meetings, centred on the theme of the analytic process, represented a unique opportunity for European and North American analysts to exchange their points of view on their 'shared tenets' and differences concerning theory and practice.

Several papers presented at various scientific meetings were published in the EPF Bulletin, *Psychoanalysis in Europe*. At the time it was a biannual *Bulletin* numbering more than a hundred pages, the format of which was modified from the autumn of 1996. The *Bulletin*'s new Editor, Gabriele Junkers, thus contributed to giving it a more attractive and readable format. It was published in the three official languages of the EPF with specific colours for each language: red for English, blue for French and green for German. This tradition is kept alive even today, 20 years later.

From this viewpoint, the *Bulletin* achieved a balance between scientific and administrative needs and could arouse the interest of analysts in a good many European countries, all the while maintaining the simplicity of an internal bulletin. On this point, it differs from a psychoanalytic journal, which aims at publishing articles on every possible subject or on a chosen theme. In an article that appeared on the occasion of the 25th anniversary of the *Bulletin*, Peter Hildebrand (1997), its founder, regretted that our publication was particularly centred on the minutes of our scientific meetings and that it was not especially open to various subjects that were not necessarily connected to the EPF's activities in accordance with the vision he himself had worked towards when the Bulletin was created.

In fact, the *Bulletin*'s evolution has followed that of the EPF: if, at its beginnings, the EPF organised only a very few scientific meetings and thus did not have to report on them, it was not the case more than two decades later and the *Bulletin* attested to this change through the publication of texts, often having a very great value, presented in the course of the EPF's meetings.

II.   Political stakes at the end of the 1990s

If the EPF objectives, according to its statutes, were principally 'the promotion of the development of psychoanalysis' and 'improvement of communication among psychoanalysts by means of publications, bulletins, scientific conferences and other meetings', as an institution its responsibilities were limited to three domains: the professional status of the psychoanalyst, the opening up to Eastern Europe and the relations between the EPF and the IPA.

a)   The professional status of the psychoanalyst

The European Federation was asked to discuss the question of the identity of psychoanalysis and the psychoanalyst in relation to international institutions bringing together psychoanalytic and/or non-psychoanalytic psychotherapies. This question assumed a particular cast in the course of the 1990s due to the intervention of the State in the legislation of the practice of psychoanalysis, and investigating the medium to long-term consequences of the *Single European Act* was no trivial matter. Gilbert Diatkine and I (1996) had worked on a broad enquiry in European psychoanalytic Societies in order to describe very precisely the differences among psychoanalysts as to their professional status.

The experience of the British Confederation of Psychotherapists, bringing together the British Psycho-analytical Society and the Associations of Psychotherapy, had shown that it was possible to promote an umbrella organisation, attributing a status of psychoanalytic psychotherapy that was not contrary to the goals of psychoanalytic Societies. This implied a refusal of any organisation that aimed at bringing together the psychotherapy associations, analytic and non-analytic; in other words, the refusal of the United Kingdom Standing Conference for Psychotherapy (UKSCP) at the national level as well as the European Association for Psychotherapy (EAP) at an international level.

From this standpoint, other countries such as Germany, the Netherlands and Switzerland had to face the hazards of financial dependence on the State with the risk of leading to a loss of psychoanalysis's identity. The case of Switzerland was exemplary with regard to a psychoanalytic Society's hesitation to commit itself, or not, to an association of psychotherapists, above all when this status determined the possibility of reimbursement by the State and the recognition of a professional status. The reimbursement system by health services was recent enough in Switzerland in so far as it was enacted in 1986. At about the same time, 18 associations of psychotherapists worked on a charter project concerning training in psychotherapy; a project in which four members of the Swiss Psychoanalytical Society participated. In 1992, the Swiss Society was asked to sign the Charter for the duration of two years. After a good many discussions, it voted in favour by a single voice. Nevertheless, in 1994, the Swiss Psychoanalytical Society decided, through a negative vote this time, to leave the Charter in order to preserve the specificity of the practice of psychoanalysis.

The debate went as follows. Is a psychoanalytic society's role thought of as scientific; is its goal to transmit psychoanalysis by giving its members and candidates the freedom and responsibility to resolve individually and autonomously the concrete aspects of the practice of psychoanalysis? Or should it seek to assume the responsibility of these concrete aspects by involving itself in the active pursuit of a policy concerning the profession? It was thus that Betty Denzler, then President of the Swiss Society, submitted the question of the Charter's vote at the Swiss Society's General Assembly (23 June 1992).

We see that the European Federation is confronted with these very questions. Should it remain a site of scientific exchange among colleagues or should it work towards the recognition of a professional status on the European level? Views differ on this debate according to each specific psychoanalytic Society: one may, as in the Netherlands, acknowledge interest in joining an association of non-analytic psychotherapists; one may, on the contrary, as in France or Switzerland, refuse this kind of affiliation; or one may, lastly, as in Great Britain, create a national or international association of psychoanalytic psychotherapists.

The option of non-regulation has the advantage of clarity and purity as it thereby preserves the private character of the psychoanalytic experience. However, the situation may not always be clear and self-evident when State regulations specifically put psychoanalytic identity into question. In fact, the idea of joining non-analytic associations of psychotherapists such as the EAP (be it the Dutch model, at the time losing momentum, or the much more active Austrian model, based on the Strasbourg Declaration) has not been especially welcomed by the psychoanalytic societies.

Just as the EAP campaigned for the recognition of the title of psychotherapist on the European level, should psychoanalysts consider grouping together with a status of psychoanalyst or, rather, join an association of psychoanalytic psychotherapists within a status of the psychoanalytic psychotherapist?

The EPF Council was never indifferent to all these questions, which it discussed for many years; and they remained on the agenda for the years to come, given the prospect aimed at by several associations of psychotherapists of a European-wide recognition of the title and the necessity of not finding ourselves in a weak position should the question be raised in future.

Although the European Union declared that it did not intend to pronounce on the project of a status of the psychotherapist and/or the psychoanalyst, it was not indifferent as to the evolution of psychotherapy societies. Indeed, it launched a wide-ranging enquiry into the legislative organisation of psychotherapeutic activities entitled 'Psychotherapies in Europe (BioMed-DG XII)'. It aimed at assessing the different systems used in the countries of the European Community, and its questions merged with those that G. Diatkine and myself had put to the psychoanalytic Societies.

The future confirmed, in France, for example, that at the beginning of the 21st century, the State had institutionalised the title of psychotherapist, which drew particularly fierce reactions from the psychoanalytic societies as they wished to remain exempt from the obligation of obtaining this title for private psychoanalytic practice. The French psychoanalytic Societies have, however, recommended that psychoanalysts practicing in an institution should request it.

b)   The development of psychoanalysis in Eastern Europe

Well before the fall of the Berlin wall in November 1989, the EPF had established close contact with psychoanalytic groups in Eastern Europe. The political evolution simply confirmed the importance of scientific backing for all colleagues who had long worked clandestinely or in isolation during the era of the Communist regimes.[2] The EPF thus mounted a Commission directed by Eero Rechardt (Finnish Society), which aimed at ensuring the coordination of aid offered to Eastern European countries. The members of this Commission were Han Groen-Prakken (Dutch Society), Michael Rotmann (German Association), Paolo Fonda (Italian Society) and Aira Laine (Finnish Society).

The EPF had a further essential role to play at the time when several Eastern European countries were still functioning at the level of a pre-study group. It served as intermediary between Western European Societies and Eastern European groups for teaching, the selection of psychiatrists and psychologists interested in training in a Western Society and, additionally, the purchase of books and psychoanalytic journals for Eastern Europeans.

In the autumn of 1989, a few weeks before the fall of the Berlin wall, the EPF began to organise a *Seminar for Eastern Europeans*, initially annual but which later took place every two years, alternating with the Summer University. The *Seminar for Eastern Europeans* was open to all Western analysts and brought together about 60 Eastern Europeans, mostly psychiatrists and psychologists interested in psychoanalysis coming from all the Eastern European countries. The Seminar represented an exceptional opportunity for Western and Eastern Europeans to meet together with the goal of discussing theoretic and clinical presentations. The *Summer University* was conceived in order to make intensive instruction available for a week to some 60 Eastern Europeans; 12 or so teachers from the West gave free instruction.

From this viewpoint the *Seminar for Eastern Europeans*, which took place in Moscow during the 1998 Whit Sunday weekend on the theme of psychoanalytic training in Central and Eastern Europe, represented a watershed in the development of psychoanalysis in Eastern European countries. Whereas we were expecting between 100 and 150 participants from the East and West combined, more than 500 participants registered and engaged in lively discussions, often overflowing with enthusiasm, on psychoanalysis. Two analysts from the West brought up the question of the differing aspects of analytic training, and representatives from the Eastern Societies (Hungary and the Czech Republic) and Groups (Lithuania and Russia) recalled the various aspects of their training experiences. In addition, training analysts from

---

2   For details on the opening up of the EPF to Eastern European countries, see Han Groen-Prakken (1997).

the West led supervision groups. The seminar marked the beginnings of the analytic renewal in Russia after the destruction by Stalin of the Russian Psychoanalytical Association, which at the turn of the 20th century had been a centre for psychoanalysis, with Russian being one of the first translations into a foreign language of one of Freud's works, in 1902.

The IPA and the EPF worked jointly to afford these groups the possibility of informing themselves about psychoanalysis and perhaps getting training in the West in good environments. The success of these annual encounters of the EPF confirmed the importance of the presence of the IPA and EPF in these countries at a time when other psychoanalytic groups not belonging to the IPA, and giving a distorted image of analytic work, declared themselves prepared to set out 'in conquest of Eastern Europe'. It was important neither to sell analytic work 'off cheap' nor to follow an ideal of 'pure' psychoanalysis. Successful training in these countries needed to be located somewhere between these two extremes. These countries very often presented a pioneering situation, just as in Freud's time, which meant that a presence had to be assured all the while taking into account the historical factors that necessitated finding exceptional means in order to face exceptional situations. It was in this context of uncertainty, in which training criteria were not always clearly defined, that in 2002 the Han Groen-Prakken Psychoanalytic Institute (PIEE), under the leadership of Paolo Fonda, was founded by the IPA in collaboration with the EPF. The principle and practice of shuttle analysis was then accepted, with a minimum criterion of one hundred sessions a year.[3]

c)   Relations between the EPF and the IPA

If in principle the differences between the EPF and the IPA were clear, it was not always the case in practice, and this was for several reasons. The project of restructuring the IPA was accepted at the beginning of the 1990s in so far as the need for representing the Societies within the IPA Executive Council in order to increase its legitimacy became clear. The principle of direct democracy in the IPA (direct election of the members of the Executive Council by the administrative Assembly and then by the entirety of the members thanks to

---

3   For a detailed narrative of the history of the Institute, see Paolo Fonda (2010).

absentee voting) was effectively called into question since, in principle, power was greater in the hands of the Executive Committee (President, General Secretary, Treasurer) than in those of the Executive Council, which only met twice yearly and was often seen as a body that passed decisions made by the Executive Committee.

These are the reasons that led both the Societies and the IPA to consider a structural reform of the IPA, which would make possible changes in institutional functioning and new policy decisions, given the necessity of a greater legitimacy for the decisions taken by the IPA.

On the level of the EPF, the European Presidents thus decided, at the Council meeting of 13 October 1988, to consider the need for EPF representation within the IPA Executive Council. A Committee presided over by James Innes-Smith, then President of the Belgian Society, was established in order to study this question.

On the IPA level, during the 1989 Rome Congress, an *Assembly of Presidents of the Component Societies* was likewise created. The first two designated secretaries of this assembly, James Innes-Smith (Belgian Society) and Pierre Fédida (French Association), were moreover European Presidents.

Furthermore, the IPA decided to create a Committee in order to study the project of a restructuring of the IPA. These different moves resulted in the following decisions. The EPF was not mandated to represent the psychoanalytic Societies with the IPA; rather, this would be done by the European presidents at the Presidents' Assembly. Moreover, the Committee for restructuring the IPA suggested creating a *House of Delegates* at the Administrative Assembly that met in July 1995 at the Amsterdam Congress; a project aimed at incorporating the Societies without turning the IPA into a federation of Societies, as was the case for the EPF. The proposal of nine delegates per continent was accepted, with the election of one delegate per continent at the IPA Executive Council; the worth of attributing, or not, a voting right to the three delegates who participated in the IPA Executive Council was examined. The decision to give them a voting right in fact constituted a step towards the idea of a federalising of the IPA.

From this time onwards, the Presidents' Assembly and the House of Delegates operated between the EPF and the IPA. Discussions took place in order to consider the relations between these different institutions. The options were then the following:

Should we move towards a Confederation of Societies through the intermediary of their regional federations, in so far as they would have an equivalent administrative status? The advantage was doubtless important with regard to the demographic increase and improved representation of the Societies within the IPA. The risk was still the possible inadequate representation of the members by their Societies' representatives.

Or should we, on the contrary, maintain the balance between the EPF, the Presidents' Assembly, the House of Delegates and the IPA in order to avoid a politicisation of the EPF and so encourage its scientific specificity? This was the option chosen by the EPF Council at the time of the changes in its structure. The future has shown that this balance has been maintained by means of the decision taken by the IPA to create, beginning in 2003, a Council of Representatives whose members are respectively elected by each of the three regions.

Conclusion

At the dawn of the 21st century, the EPF was confronted with a redefinition of its place in relation to the other international psychoanalytic Societies and analytic institutions. Could we maintain a clear distinction between the scientific and the political? Certain problems encountered showed that the distinction was not always natural, in particular concerning training in general and training in Eastern Europe in particular. All EPF activities sought to promote the identity of psychoanalysis and psychoanalysts, taking into account the diversity of cultures, languages and traditions. Rather than being an obstacle, such diversity should have contributed to the enrichment of European psychoanalysis, on the condition however of preserving the 'experience of the unconscious', the precise guarantor of our identity.

This is the reason why the EPF planned to consider in particular the problems of thought and languages in Europe and thus created to this end a Commission presided over by Jacqueline Amati-Mehler (Italian Association). The Commission presented the results of its initial research to the spring 1998 EPF Council meeting. Likewise, also in 1998, the EPF Scientific Symposium, whose theme was communication among psychoanalysts, demonstrated that in an era when we were transitioning from use of the fax to the internet, it was important to think more than ever about how European psychoanalysts communicated with each other. Throughout the 1990s, this was a veritable revolution, a time when psychoanalytic Societies had gradually to decide if they were going to purchase a fax machine in order to facilitate exchanges between institutions and members of our Societies. We surely crack a smile when we think back to the 1990s when the EPF sent faxes to the Presidents and might even wake them in the middle of the night if they had carelessly left their machines on in their bedrooms! But a sign that the times were changing was when Gabriele Junkers, then Editor of the *Bulletin*, proudly announced in the autumn 1998 issue of *Psychoanalysis in Europe* (Bulletin 51) that the EPF now had at its disposal a website!

Important questions remained to be asked, in particular concerning finances, since the cost of the *Bulletin* and the arrival of a good many Eastern European countries in the Council had called into question the health of our association's budget. Moreover, the diversity of our European meetings satisfied the need for Europeans to work in small groups, but a degree of weariness and repetition began to be felt among participants. A change was necessary, which my successor David Tuckett well understood, and he decided to bring all these exchanges together into a single annual congress, rather than happening every two years, in addition to creating the European Working Parties. This would be the experience for the decade to come.

Translated from the French by Steven Jaron, Paris.

References

DIATKINE, G., & GIBEAULT, A. (1996). The status of psychotherapist and/or psychoanalyst. *Psychoanalysis in Europe* (46), 114–143.

DIATKINE, R., FREUD, A., & SEGAL, H. (1972). Symposium organised by the EPF on 'The Role of Child Analysis in Psychoanalytic Training'. *Int. J. Psychoanal. 53*(1).

FONDA, P. (2010), A virtual training institute in Europe. *Psychoanalysis in Europe* (64 suppl.).

GROEN-PRAKKEN, H. (1997). Towards a pan-European psychoanalytical federation: On the development of the psychoanalytic movement in Central and Eastern Europe, 1987–1996. *Psychoanalysis in Europe* (48), 5–23.

HILDEBRANDT, P. (1997). Founding of the Bulletin of the EPF. *Psychoanalysis in Europe* (48), 24–26.

2000–2004: The New Scientific Policy and the Ten Year Scientific Initiative

David Tuckett

I became EPF President in November 1999, unexpectedly and in sad circumstances after an emergency election. It was caused by the sudden death of the President-Elect, Jim Innes Smith (from Belgium) in January that year, and was traumatic. Jim had done nearly a year of work preparing to take over from Alain Gibeault and had been due to start in March. I did not know him well, but we had talked about European psychoanalysis and scientific exchange in Wiesbaden at the German conference. Suddenly there was grief, anxiety and a vacuum and it was against this background that the then-EPF Bulletin Editor, Gabriele Junkers, asked me on her behalf, and also of others in France and Germany, if I would stand. I said I'd think about it. By the time I had said yes it turned out there were already two candidates so we would be three. I had been to EPF conferences and found them serious and worthwhile but I knew very little about the organisation. The other two candidates, on the other hand, were from the Executive and had been doing important work in the Federation.

The people who vote in EPF elections are the Presidents of the European Societies and also (at that time but not since) the six members of the Executive. In thinking whether to accept nomination I thought quite hard about what might be the main purpose of an international federation and decided that it was to meet and exchange ideas in a facilitating atmosphere where the aim was to try *to improve the standard of our psychoanalytic work*.

My election statement (which can be found in the online version of this paper) stressed my wish to build on my good experience of EPF events, my accumulation of knowledge as Editor of the IJP team and my clinical experience working with analytic cases, in order to further develop EPF as a place for first-rate scientific exchange based on clear argument and evidence. I argued that the EPF was not for politics and that the main task was to work at understanding how best to do analysis, to promote analysis, to make training effective and to understand analysis. I also suggested that while pluralism and tolerance are greatly to be welcomed in the face of previous dogma, we risked becoming muddled. I then suggested that respect of all views was necessary but that we needed which had to start with being prepared to make choices based on the scientifically based arguments that can be marshalled and the facts supporting them.

I think about two-thirds of the presidents voted for me but only five of the Executive so it was close.

Once elected I appointed Gabriele Junkers (ending her term as *Bulletin* Editor) as EPF Secretary and in February 2000 the new Executive met in Madrid for a long discussion. At first it was very hard for everyone. Gabriele and the newly appointed *Bulletin* Editor, Eike Wolff, were new, and enthusiastic about what I had suggested. But one of the four members from the old Executive had been a candidate in the election and two had been strongly in favour of him or the other candidate. There was mistrust and resentment. However, after a very difficult and frank interchange for two hours, the six of us had dinner around a very beautiful oval table in a very elegant private dining room organised by our Madrid colleagues. We ate a magnificent sea bass cooked in a block of salt! The next evening around midnight, the then-President of the Madrid Society took us to an extraordinarily erotic performance at one of the oldest flamenco clubs deep in a Madrid cellar! She knew the owner and it was enlivening.

By the end of the weekend we had concluded a working discussion. I insisted that I had been elected to try and implement a policy but that this policy was not to be imposed from thin air but to take off from where the Federation was from the previous hard work and from what the presidents wanted to do. Gradually we developed a working atmosphere to which everyone contributed. I remember Emma Piccioli (Vice President) discussing new ways of organising the conference of the Italian Society and Imre Szecsody (Vice President) and Henk Jan Dalewijk (Treasurer) talking about the need to include research. Gabriele and Eike had ideas about moving to email (until then it was faxes and letters) and creating a website for the EPF, and so on.

We formulated what was to become the EPF's 'New Scientific Policy', which I drafted from the notes of the discussion on the plane home. I sent it round the next day and after iterations it was put to the Council at its meeting in London in April and strongly supported after a lengthy discussion. The details are in the *Bulletin*[1]. There was a set of general central ideas about the need to set priorities and that these would be to design our meetings and activities to find ways to work in depth, to learn better from each other, to develop motivation and rigorous self-sustaining initiatives, to meet as much as possible in small groups, to set and monitor objectives as to how far we were improving mutual understanding, and to adopt increased peer reviewed publication as outcome criteria. Work was also to be more focused and to try to develop year on year. There were four specific focuses to work at: improved clinical work, improved educational activity, better theoretical clarification of differences and better linking of our discipline to 'problems, concepts and structures in the wider world'. Additionally, there were some organisation reforms, aimed at increasing the power and responsibility of the presidents of the Societies and their potential effectiveness in the IPA.

Conferences are organised far ahead so there was only time to introduce a few new elements into the Madrid conference. The first 'new style' conference took place in Prague in 2002. Henk Jan and I visited more than 20 hotels and even the former Communist Party HQ in a single day one cold January in 2001 before finding a place where we could have plenary meetings and lots of small groups. I learned from Henk Jan how to assess a hotel in ten minutes – for instance, insist on seeing behind by going down the emergency stairs and keep the conversation for the bar area so you can assess how management get on with staff! We also earned that facilities for a 'new style' small group conference ran counter to the big auditoria and 'keep them controlled' philosophies then prevailing and that specialist conference organisers were an expensive liability, especially if they didn't know our ways.

Eventually the Prague conference was attended by large numbers of enthusiastic participants who had not been to meetings before and featured many small groups, among them those organised by the four new working parties seeking to make progress in our clinical and theoretical thinking, edu-

---

1   Available at: http://www.epf-fep.eu/eng/article/the-epf-policy-and-objectives-for-
    the-next-few-years

cation and interface. It was the first conference in the areas previously behind the Iron Curtain and in consultation with our Czech colleagues we focused on the external world and its impact on the internal, looking especially at the impact of the Holocaust. Betty Joseph gave the final address. More details of that conference and the next two 'new style' conferences in Sorrento and Helsinki can be found in the online *Bulletin* that dates from that time, including a detailed description of the developing philosophy and the five working parties to that date.[2]

What gradually happened is conveniently summed up in the words of Evelyne Sechaud, one of the architects of how things developed when she joined the Executive as Vice President in 2001. In her opening remarks[3] as the incoming President at the EPF conference in Portugal, three years later in 2005, she said:

> The New Style is now the style of the EPF conference. It is composed of two streams: one with a main theme consisting of several panels which allow for debate on theoretical views and clinical material; and the other with five working parties including the Working Party on Theoretical Issues chaired by Jorge Canestri, the Working Party on Comparative Clinical Methods chaired by David Tuckett, the Working Party on Education chaired by Gabriele Junkers, the Working Party on Interface chaired by Shmuel Erlich, and the Working Party on Initiating Psychoanalysis chaired by Bernard Reith. Included in the second stream are the Forum on Clinical Issues, chaired by Haydée Faimberg and several ad hoc groups and other events. This very important stream, which has existed for the past four years, mainly permits work to take place in small groups. This allows many colleagues to participate more actively in the meetings and to become more involved in the scientific initiatives of the EPF, which, globally, aim to confront the crisis in psychoanalysis.

The success and enthusiasm of the working parties, which by 2003 were already involving some one hundred people in the inner core of people working

2   Building a Psychoanalysis Based in Confidence in What We Do. Available at: http://www.epf-fep.eu/eng/article/building-a-psychoanalysis-based-on-confidence-in-what-we-do
3   Available at: http://www.epf-fep.eu/eng/article/opening-presidential-address-to-interpret-to-translate

hard for twelve months each year and three times that number attending the workshops they organised at the conference, led my Executive to propose to the Council at its 2003 meeting what was called the Ten Year Scientific Initiative[4]. The initiative was aimed at what was being discussed at IPA level as a crisis in psychoanalysis – namely the:

> ... undeniable fact: that in nearly all established European countries (as in most other places worldwide) there are fewer patients than we would wish willing to undertake full psychoanalysis and fewer candidates (especially those in their twenties and thirties) wanting to train as psychoanalysts. This trend, unless it is arrested, threatens the future of psychoanalysis. If graduates from psychoanalytic institutes cannot be assured true psychoanalytic work of the kind they have been trained to do, they and their families may doubt the wisdom of training or may opt for some other less demanding option.

We called on the IPA to accept that 'facilitating and realizing a solution to this crisis should be the primary task of the IPA Executive, the new Board and Committees' and that 'All activities and the allocation of the resources are to be considered according to their relevance in addressing this problem' and that each IPA region 'should develop its plan to counter the situation and the IPA should make funds available to support these plans.'[5] (We weren't successful with the IPA and neither was I later when although twice elected to the Board with overwhelming support from European members I failed miserably to persuade it either to reduce its bureaucracy or to take educational and clinical standards seriously. Actually they are not really ever discussed).

The ten-year initiative for the EPF was accepted by the EPF Council (with only one abstention) at a meeting the day after the Sorrento conference in 2003. The initiative proposed that in the next ten years we should focus and concentrate our activities on aspiring to achieve twelve reasonably ambitious objectives:

---

4   Available at: http://www.epf-fep.eu/eng/article/a-ten-year-european-scientific-initia tive-presidential-address
5   David Tuckett, *Bulletin* 57, 2003, pp. 7–21. Available at: http://www.epf-fep.eu/eng/ar ticle/a-ten-year-european-scientific-initiative-presidential-address

1. *Formally describing the types of working psychoanalytically.* We need to have developed a list of clearly described and identifiable 'best practice' ways of working psychoanalytically, written down and illustrated by clinical examples in as great a depth as possible, covering the main types of doing psychoanalysis in an acceptable manner in Europe. Based on this information it should be possible to decide into which type any description of a psychoanalysis falls. It should also be possible to say when work does not fall into any of these categories (e. g. when it should be regarded as an innovation or as not a way of doing psychoanalysis, according to whatever argument is set out).

2. *Assessing the effectiveness of working psychoanalytically.* We should aspire to reach at least preliminary and transparent conclusions (arrived at in psychoanalytically appropriate ways, yet to be determined and debated but which convince us) as to the comparative evidence for the effect of each type of working on the problems presented by different kinds of patients.

3. *Creating a patient referral and diagnosis programme.* We should have built up a committed expert group of clinical workers in each country with developed skills (and written and research publications) for assessing patients for psychoanalysis and determining the conditions for advising psychoanalytic treatment.

4. *Creating transparent means to assess training outcomes.* We need to have achieved an agreed set of transparent criteria to assess competence in conducting each type of working, which would be suitable to determine when a candidate's training has successfully achieved its objective.

5. *Publishing studies of the effectiveness of different educational systems.* We should have published detailed studies of the relative effects of different training and continuing professional development programmes.

6. *Creating an established body of outreach programme expertise.* We should have established and described in writing a series of programmes covering public education, liaison with other professionals (including psychotherapists, counsellors, psychologists, social workers, physicians and psychiatrists) and work with referral agencies and have made some effort to monitor and to report their effectiveness.

7. *Establishing a peer-review-culture tradition at the EPF conference.* We should have achieved a noticeably different peer culture that puts for-

ward ideas and gets rigorous feedback at European psychoanalytic meetings – so that, for example, presenting papers on work in progress and attending the EPF conference to offer comment on these papers becomes a high-status competitive achievement valued among us, with the papers being regularly accepted for publication in peer-reviewed journals, following revision.

8. *Creating ongoing communicating peer groups.* We should have established groups of colleagues with the time and inclination to be more than just clinicians and we should support and value them. We need to have established core groups of 100 or so committed research workers, 100 committed outreach workers, 100 committed research clinicians, and 100 committed training analysts, all getting to know and trust and respect each other: meeting regularly, exchanging ideas, and being aware of one another's work on the above topics, based on critical peer review.

9. *Creating university links.* We should know exactly how and where psychoanalysis is being taught in universities in Europe and have established a fellowship programme to create the conditions for a significant number of full-time psychoanalysts to engage in university-based research work and for a significant number of university research workers to be involved in joint projects with psychoanalysts.

10. *Establishing peer-reviewed publication as the norm.* We should have achieved the publication of at least 100 papers based on this work programme in peer-reviewed journals.

11. *Creating some university-based psychoanalytic training.* Within ten years, institutes in all those countries where it is considered desirable (and I accept that in some countries it will not be) should be qualifying some psychoanalytic candidates who have been selected and trained to a satisfactory level of competence in a public university degree context.

12. *Creating the means to improve referral to full psychoanalysis and regularly monitoring the demand for practice and for training.* Methods should be devised and implemented, based on the achievements above, to create ways to improve referrals for full psychoanalysis and to share them among practitioners.

At the time, apart from for proposal 11, there was not only agreement and enthusiasm but also a strong commitment to such a programme. Evelyne Sechaud was elected unanimously as President-Elect at the same meeting and at the next Council meeting set out her vision for implementation – stating that she:

> wished to emphasise the role of the Working Parties because I assume that the Conference will become increasingly the mouthpiece of the W. P. ... They have been the happy initiative ... To my viewpoint the W. P. are increasingly going to be the heart of scientific work. They are novel places for study then research (as well empirical as fundamental researches).

The annual budget for all working parties was set at €119,000 for 2004 and the success of the new style conferences and the superb financial efforts of Henk Jan Dalewijk, and then Duveken Engels, meant that in addition, the 2004 Council was able to set aside a reserve of €500,000 to the European Scientific Initiative (ESI). It was to be spent so that we could fund working parties to implement the Ten-Year Initiative. If the IPA could be persuaded by the European presidents to re-focus its priorities the scale of investment might be increased.

Evelyne Sechaud asked me to stay on to lead one working party and Gabriele Junkers to stay on and lead another. But, in fact, over the following ten years the ESI and the Ten-Year objectives were gradually dropped. Working parties got marginalised or turned into something very different from 'work'. The initiative became increasingly controversial. Somehow, it was all somehow confused with issues of power and personality – the initiative apparently being viewed as some kind of effort by an unelected clique to take over and divert the EPF from the true path of psychoanalysis and even to prevent subsequent presidents and executives from having their own policies.

Looking back, I think those who attended workshops arranged by the different working parties knew that, despite their ambitions, they were far from perfect. For those who chaired them (all originally selected by Council) it was hard work. Nonetheless, participation was rewarding. Many of the working parties were copied across the world. The concerns that drove them concerned deep issues in psychoanalysis and how to capture and understand unconscious functioning. On the plus side, four of the original five working parties are still functioning and have led to several monographs and papers, some recently published in the *International Journal* (see below). Regrettably, Interface as a topic dropped out.

I do not understand how working parties became so controversial in the EPF, particularly among those who did not attend them. Nor do I understand why their future development became so fraught with emotion and personal politics. Maybe the initiative was too ambitious and too provocative. It started from the idea that the *status quo* was not an option for long-term survival. And indeed the problems the Ten-Year initiative was designed to tackle remain; perhaps they are even more serious. Of course, they can still be picked up and so perhaps new ways implementing the initiative will emerge in due course.

I very much enjoyed my time as President. One of the main reasons for this was the work done by Gabriele Junkers. She took on the role of keeping close to the concerns of the European Society presidents and especially took on the task of encouraging them to speak. Most presidents attend the Council only four times (over two years) and very few of them have English as a mother tongue. It is a situation in which misunderstanding is waiting to happen. We wanted to involve the presidents so that they in turn would involve their membership and find new younger people to contribute. By chance the first Council meeting had been arranged in London and during it I held three small dinners in my home or small restaurants near where were meeting so that I could meet personally all the presidents. Afterwards, Gabriele kept in touch with many of them (by phone and personal visits) and we tried to help the new ones (who would join each six months) to understand what was going on – an organisation in which the governing council is nearly completely different after three meetings is a very challenging one if people were to be active not passive participants.

Perhaps we were successful at involving presidents and facilitating their participation. I hope so and, if so, it was a great deal down to Gabriele. She worked tirelessly before and after meetings to make sure people were involved, continuously opening channels of communication and trying to anticipate people's needs and concerns. I am deeply grateful to her, to all my Executive colleagues over those years and to all the European presidents of that time. I think we enjoyed what we were doing and thought what we were part of was useful. They were stimulating times and fun. We did not achieve the main objective but we met lots of people we had never met, learned a lot about each other's ways of working psychoanalytically, using the twenty or so languages and traditions in Europe, and hopefully improved our own and some others' clinical work.

Some references to work from the working parties

BASILE, R., BIRKSTED BREEN, D., BONARD, O., DENIS, P., DIERCKS, M., FERRO, A., HEBBRECHT, M., HINZE, E., JACKSON, D. J., MARIOTTI, P., MAUSS HANKE, A., & TUCKETT, D. (2010). How do psychoanalysts work? The work of the EPF working party on comparative clinical methods 2003–2009. *EPF Bulletin 64* (Suppl), 5–32.

BONARD, O. (2011). Methodical Clinical Comparison: Where are we and what are our projects? Analytic styles and metapsychology. Report of the Working Party on Comparative Clinical Methods (WPCCM). *EPF Bulletin 65*, 28–29.

CANESTRI, J. (2006). *Psychoanalysis: From Practice to Theory*. London, John Wiley.

CRICK, P. (2014). Selecting a patient or initiating a psychoanalytic process? *Int. J. Psychoanal.* doi. 10.1111/1745–8315.12142.

ERLICH-GINOR, M. (2010). Working party on education. *EPF Bulletin 64* (Suppl.), 33–56.

ERLICH-GINOR, M., & ERLICH, S. (2014). Who is afraid of psychoanalytic evaluation? *IJP Open 1*.

HINZE, E. (2015). What do we learn in psychoanalytic training? *Int. J. Psychoanal.* 96, 755–771.

JUNKERS, G., TUCKETT, D., & ZACHRISSON, A. (2008). To be or not to be a psychoanalyst – How do we know a candidate is ready to qualify? Difficulties and controversies in evaluating psychoanalytic competence. *Psychoanal. Inq. 28*, 288–308.

LAGERLÖF, S., & SIGRELL, B. (1999). A discussion of models for the selection of patients for supervised psychoanalysis. *J. Clin. Psychoanal. 8*, 149–172.

MØLLER, M. (2014). The analyst's anxieties in the first interview: Barriers against analytic presence. *Int. J. Psychoanal.* doi: 10.1111/1745–8315.12178.

NORMAN, J., & SALOMONSSON, B. (2005). 'Weaving thoughts': A method for presenting and commenting psychoanalytic case material in a peer group. *Int. J. Psychoanal. 86*, 1281–1298.

REITH, B. (2010). The specific dynamics of initial interviews: Switching the level, or opening up a meaning space? *EPF Bulletin 64* (Suppl. EPF Working Parties)

REITH, B. (2012). What interpsychic conditions lead to full analysis? Some findings from the working party on initiating psychoanalysis. Part 1: The analyst's internal frame. *EPF Bulletin 66*, 94–102.

REITH, B. (2013). Complementary models of the mind in Freud's The unconscious? In S. Akhtar & M. K. O'Neil (Eds.), *Freud's 'The Unconscious.' Contemporary Freud: Turning points and critical issues*, 179–202. London: Karnac.

REITH, B., BOOTS, J., CRICK, P., GIBEAULT, A., JAFFE, R., LAGERLÖF, S., MØLLER, M., SKALE, E., VERMOTE, R., & WEGNER, P. (2010). The specific dynamics of initial interviews: Switching the level, or opening up a meaning space? Report on Phase 1 of the WPIP study of initial interviews. *EPF Bulletin 64* (Suppl.), 57–80.

REITH, B., LAGERLÖF, S., CRICK, P., MØLLER, M., & SKALE, E. (Eds.) (2012). *Initiating Psychoanalysis: Perspectives* (pp. 261–271). London: Routledge.

REITH, B. (2015). The first interview: anxieties and research on initiating psychoanalysis. *Int. J. Psychoanal. 96*, 637–657.

SALOMONSSON, B. (2012). Psychoanalytic case presentations in a weaving thoughts group: On countertransference and group dynamics. *Int. J. Psychoanal. 93,* 917–937.

TARGET, M. (2001). Some issues in psychoanalytical training: an overview of the literature and some resulting observations. Paper presented at the 2nd Joseph Sandler Research Conference at University College of London, 10 March.

TARGET, M. (2003). Über psychoanalytische Ausbildung: Literaturübersicht und Beobachtungen. *Forum der Psychoanalyse 19,* 193–210.

TUCKETT, D. (2002). Presidential address: The new style conference and developing a peer culture in European psychoanalysis. *EPF Bulletin 56,* 32–46.

TUCKETT, D. (2003). Presidential address: A ten year European scientific initiative. *EPF Bulletin 57,* 7–22.

TUCKETT, D. (2004). Presidential address: Building a psychoanalysis based on confidence in what we do. *EPF Bulletin 58,* 5–20.

TUCKETT, D. (2005). Does anything go?: Towards a framework for the more transparent assessment of psychoanalytic competence. *Int. J. Psychoanal. 86*(1), 31–49.

TUCKETT, D. (2011). Some reflections on psychoanalytic technique: In need of core concepts or an archaic ritual? *Psychoanal. Inq. 32,* 87–108.

TUCKETT, D., BASILE, R., BIRKSTED BREEN, D., BOHM, T., DENIS, P., FERRO, A., HINZ, H., JEMSTEDT, A., MARIOTTI, P., & SCHUBERT, J. (2008). *Psychoanalysis Comparable and Incomparable. The Evolution of a Method to Describe and Compare Psychoanalytic Approaches.* New Library of Psychoanalysis. London and New York: Routledge.

Some Thoughts on the Life of Psychoanalysis in Europe from the Point of View of a Former EPF President

Evelyne Sechaud

During my presidency of the APF (Association Psychanayltique de France) (1998–2000), the general political line I adopted could be summarised in one word – openness: the openness of my Society towards other Societies, in France and abroad; wider communication with other modes of theoretical and clinical thinking; and rediscovering at the institutional level the discovery of the other that characterises analytic thinking. A few years later, the same approach led me to become President of the EPF (2004–2008). Being President of the EPF was an extremely rich experience for me in spite of the workload and the internal tensions that are aroused by the conflicts of a large group. The President is always the object of projections, and sometimes idealisations; in any case, he or she is the privileged locus of transferences, narcissistic in particular. These well-known phenomena are obviously unanalysable in this context.

Today, more than ever, the internationalisation of psychoanalysis (and, in the near future, its globalisation) brings into play our capacities for openness at the same time as the vital interest of preserving our often-threatened identity. For me, the best guarantee of the survival of psychoanalysis lies in the firm assurance of the singular and specific identity of analytic thinking at the theoretical and clinical level, as well as at the level of the training of analysts.

But the EPF is also a large institution, which is forever developing and whose growth since my years as president has increased constantly.

Although the EPF does not have the political vocation of the IPA, it is nonetheless caught up in politics (the political thing). How? Politics, according to its most straightforward and original definition is nothing other than 'that which is related to the organisation and exercise of power within an organised society.'[1] Politics, then, is the art and practice of conducting public affairs. No organised group escapes it. And the more it believes it can, the more it is caught up in a system of varied and variable forces. The difficulty encountered by any large organisation concerns the political choices and orientation in the domain in question. Leading the group involves exercising power, which in turn depends on the varied forms of democracy, but also on the temptations of personal power, all in the context of power struggles. What are the issues at stake and their manifestations in the EPF? The major issues are of two kinds: either they concern questions of the political history of the European Union or the more specific questions of the evolution of psychoanalysis in its diverse practices and theories.

How does the EPF manage its politics in general?

In fact, the EPF – and this was one of the first surprises I had – reproduces the splits or the alliances that are formed (or undone) in the states of the European Union. I was very naïve to think that analysts could rise above the politics of the states! In fact, the movements are parallel, and the presidents of the Societies often reproduce the political movements of their respective states. This is how splits between North and South, the systems of alliances of variable geometry between the large Societies: the British with the Northern countries, the Dutch or the Germans; the French with the Germans; and above all Spain and Italy manifest themselves. The position of Eastern European countries is often linked to their evolution following their liberation from Soviet influence.

The election of the members of the Executive, as well as the adoption of initiatives by the elected Executive, can be the field where these power struggles are carried out.

Conflicts between the large and small Societies can be just as sharp. Each Society has a vote, irrespective of its size. But the large Societies regularly call this arrangement into question because it does not take into account the

---

1   The French Dictionary, *Le Petit Robert*.

number of their members, as is the case for the states of the European Union. This is especially true in that subscriptions at the EPF apply to each member, via his/her society. The mass of subscriptions paid by each society is thus proportional to the number of its members.

There is conflict, too, between the Societies of the rich countries of Western Europe and those of countries that suffer from economic and financial difficulties: formerly the Eastern countries of the Soviet group, today the countries of the Eastern Mediterranean. The participation of these Societies in the scientific activities of the EPF has often been made difficult by travelling expenses (hotels, etc.) and inscription fees.

Economic questions are equally at the heart of debates on the practice of psychotherapies and/or the systems of reimbursing analyses for specific periods. These questions, which have been dealt with in different ways by the various European states until now, are becoming more harmonised within the Union, though this is still far from being realised. Scientific discussions on these questions are consequently caught up in the constraints, the functioning or disfunctioning of the politics of the respective states.

The EPF and questions of training

From the beginnings of its existence, one of the main goals of the EPF was to make it possible for European analysts to get together to reflect on questions relating to training, didactic analysis, the selection of candidates, and supervisions. The meetings devoted to these subjects have been maintained and still have an important audience today. But the climate has changed a lot, owing to the recognition by the IPA of three models of training: the Eitingon model, the French model, and the Uruguayan model. During his presidency of the IPA, Daniel Widlöcher worked hard to obtain this result. This recognition was officially adopted in July 2005 during the Rio Congress and the handover of the presidency from Daniel Widlöcher to Claudio Eizirik. Europeans were obviously at the heart of this question. The Eitingon model and the French model are clearly differentiated, even if, today, some Societies only adopt this or that aspect of one of the models. One of the major points of interest of the Forum on Education, which continues to be held each year, is precisely that it furthers understanding of the modifications introduced by the Societies to the initial models, both to the French model and to the Eitingon model, given that training practices have been constantly evolving since the early days. But these changes also raise the question of evaluating how far each model retains its coherence and its specificity.

The recognition of these models has made it possible to get beyond the old and very lively debates in which I participated, concerning the weekly frequency of sessions required to qualify as an analysis, whether a training analysis or supervised analyses. For the Eitingon model, four or five sessions a week were required, whereas the French practised analysis on the basis of three sessions a week. This quantitative criterion, which was convenient because it could be objectified, put the accent on a criterion of objective reality that did not have much to do with the *analytic process,* the sole guarantee of the quality of an analysis, whether it is a training analysis or a personal analysis (see Jorge Canestri's report to the Congrès Psychanalytique de Langue Française [CPLF] in 2004 on the process). We know very well that the process does not depend on the number of sessions per week, provided, however, that there is a minimal frequency that not only permits the transference to be established (which can be instantaneous or, on the contrary, the object of massive resistance), but above all its analysis. The lower frequency in the French model was the object of reflections and often very sharp criticism concerning two important aspects of the process: regression and continuity. But which regression? Where are we putting the emphasis? On temporal regression, which facilitates the emergence of infantile sexuality and actualises object-relations or on topographical and formal regression, images and dreams, both of which are combined in fantasies? Such a question brings into play different metapsychological theorisations and conceptions. The same is true for the question of the necessary continuity of the sessions. How do we believe an analysis unfolds? Does it involve reconstructing an infantile neurosis or putting the history of the subject into narrative form? How much value do we ascribe to the dimension of *après-coup (Nachträglichkeit, 'deferred action')*? And if the number of sessions remains an essential element of the setting, how much importance do we give to the other parameters that also constitute a guarantee of the continuity of the process, such as the permanence and reliability of the setting, and the rule concerning the payment of missed sessions? Likewise, how much importance do we give to the fundamental rule of free association, which allows for the emergence of the unexpected, of the *Einfall,* everything that puts the discourse to rout. All these questions meet with different answers depending on the major metapsychological orientations of analysts, and our training modalities bear traces of them. It is this permanent confrontation that seems to me to be extremely fruitful in international discussions; it is not a matter, of course, of convincing or of converting those who think differently from ourselves, but of making it possible to question the foundations of our convictions and to strengthen our identity. This is how we will continue to transmit the psychoanalytic heritage.

The position of psychoanalysis in the world today

It is customary today to denounce the crisis of psychoanalysis. My predecessor, David Tuckett, had based his policy on denouncing this crisis and had suggested ways of struggling against it. The situation did not improve during my mandate and we are no doubt facing a deep cultural and social crisis. Contemporary culture has integrated psychoanalysis, which continues to arouse curiosity. A weekly magazine has only to devote an issue to psychoanalysis for its sales to shoot up sharply. But this media coverage has been accompanied by a watering-down, an 'assimilation' in which the subversive force of the unconscious and of Freudian discovery has been lost. Psychoanalysis finds itself in competition with other, shorter, 'lighter', and more targeted therapeutic modalities and has found itself summoned to provide evidence of its efficacy (see studies by Rolf Sandell in Sweden and Marianne Leuzinger-Bohleber in Germany).

The crisis is also raging *within* psychoanalysis, and analysts themselves are contributing to making it worse. Within contemporary psychoanalysis, we have witnessed the development of a plurality of theories and practices. Psychoanalysis is now applied to a large range of non-neurotic psycho-pathological organisations, which raise challenging questions both clinically and conceptually and challenge the creative capacities of analysts. The conditions of the setting have diversified, the number of sessions, face-to-face sessions, the use of new media (internet, Skype, telephone), to make psychoanalysis accessible for analysands or candidates who are at a distance geographically: in Asia, for example.

The Freudian theory of psychic functioning is under attack from the neurosciences. Questions about the scientificity of psychoanalysis are constantly renewed. In a certain number of theoretical developments, there is a tendency for metapsychology to disappear in favour of the intersubjective or interpersonal relationship. The unconscious, the drive, infantile sexuality, psychic reality, the modifications introduced by the dimension of *après-coup* (*Nachträglichkeit, 'deferred action'*) are supplanted by the reality of early relationships and traumatisms of all kinds. What has become of Freudian doctrine today? The issues at stake for the future of psychoanalysis are considerable. The confrontation of theories and practices helps us to understand deviations from the fundamental concepts, but also to re-centre our researches in psychoanalysis on the specificity of psychoanalytic treatment today. Treatment is to be understood in its double sense of referring both to a therapeutic modality and the transformation of unconscious and drive-related material. The Working Party created in 2006 on my initiative had the aim, precisely, of identifying the specificity of analytic listening beyond differences of theories and practices. The result of the analytic process is evaluated in terms of the characteristics of individual and group psychic productivity (in the context of small groups of psychoanalysts from different analytic cultures).

What remains of the unconscious?

Let's take the example of the unconscious, which could be regarded as our common denominator. During the EPF Congress of 2004 (in Helsinki), we saw how the apparently consensual reference to this central concept, truly a cornerstone of psychoanalysis, masks important differences in Europe in our clinical practice, in our theoretical elaborations, and in our training models. The choice of this theme was intended to be provocative. Reflecting on this theme was a way of rediscovering the subversive value of psychoanalysis!

The Freudian unconscious is indeed in itself a provocation: it is a category that asserts itself in its negativity and whose normal or pathological formations question and stimulate in us all the search for a meaning that might be attributed to dreams, slips, symptoms, and the transference. But the means of approach that aims at its discovery is far from natural. On 4 August 1916, Lou Andreas Salomé wrote to Freud, who had complained about the halting advances in his research:

The question is one of knowing how far the investigation into the object of your research, the Unconscious, inevitably involves the necessity of only letting itself be approached through these interruptions ... For however scientific the method of investigation is, the unconscious will always tend to elude it, just as dreams elude us on waking. It will always require an almost unnatural exertion to dedicate oneself to this subject.

It is indeed an unnatural exertion, which has to overcome resistances. A few years ago (in a little book called *L'ombre de l'objet* [The Shadow of the Object, 1990], Marie Moscovici suggested a metaphor that I rather like. She compared the work of analytic investigation to the way salmon move forward! When spawning, salmon go up river, against the current, towards the source. Going against the natural slope of repression or indeed denial, with the effort and tenacity that this implies – this, then, is what the unconscious and the sexuality that prompts it imposes on us! It is a dynamic unconscious, constantly in movement, which attracts, repels, finds paths of access, and favours detours. But what a pleasure it is, too, when a flash of 'insight' suddenly makes accessible this bit of the unknown, which, from being strange and troubling, may then become familiar! It is also a pleasure to discover, retrospectively, what had hitherto been impeding the inner freedom to think, to love, to work ...

However, in Freud's work, the unconscious does not always have the same status, passing from a system opposed to the Preconscious-Conscious to a quality that characterises the essence of psychic life. Today, across the different psychoanalytic currents represented in Europe, how do we use this reference to the unconscious in our clinical work, in our theoretical elaboration, and in our training models?

For Freud, dreams were the 'royal road' of the discovery of the unconscious. In 1900, in *The Interpretation of Dreams (Traumdeutung)* (1900a), Freud identifies the characteristic processes of the unconscious, the primary processes (opposed to the secondary processes of conscious thinking): displacement, condensation, symbolisation. In 1915, he added other aspects: the ignorance of time, negation, and contradiction. Among other formations of the unconscious (slips, bungled actions [Fehlleistungen], symptoms), the dream, or rather the dream narrative, had a special place, since it provided the model of the analytic session: with his free-floating attention the analyst follows the movements of thought, deconstructs the discourse, does the work of secondary elaboration in the reverse direction in order to discover through a formal and topographical regression the functioning of the primary processes and unconscious representation. Interpretation corresponds, then, to the definition Freud gives of it when he opposes it to construction: short, incisive, directed at an isolated element. The *'Witz'* can be the model for this. What has become today of that type of analysis which places the accent on the intrapsychic and the metapsychology of the unconscious? It is based on the first topography and neurotic functioning.

The content of the unconscious is essentially constituted (apart from the primal repressed) of repressed infantile sexual representations that are are mobilised by the the actuality of the transference. Unconscious phantasy, which Freud conceives of as a scenario, stages unconscious desire but in a secondarised form, which makes it a 'mixed blood': a mixture of unconscious and preconscious. With Melanie Klein, unconscious phantasy assumes a more primitive form by becoming the psychical representative of the drive. Unconscious desire strives towards its fulfilment according to the pleasure principle and seeks to thwart repression which keeps it out of the Preconscious-Conscious. Conflict is intersystemic and manifests itself in the treatment through resistances, which indicate the strength of the repression. Desire implies a representation that can present itself *(Darstellen)* in different forms, hallucinatory or symbolic. In the unconscious it is a question of thing-presentations, which must link up with word-presentations to become conscious. Language plays an essential role here. Language has a special importance in Francophone psychoanalysis. What other paths of access to the unconscious can be valued by other analytic cultures?

In his essay of 1915 on the unconscious, Freud concludes that the analysis of the psychoses 'promises to furnish us with conceptions through which the enigmatic Unconscious will be brought more within our reach, and, as it were, made tangible" (1915a, p. 196). In schizophrenia, words are subjected to the primary process. Words prevail over thing-presentations and the substitutions operated concern verbal identity and not the similarity of the things designated. In psychotic thinking words are taken for things. What has the analysis of the psychoses since Freud contributed to our knowledge of the unconscious?

With the second topography, the unconscious becomes an adjective which qualifies the essential aspects of the mind. The id becomes coextensive with the unconscious of the first topography, but a large part of the ego as well as the superego/ego ideal are equally unconscious. The id leaves no place for representation; it is the seat of the drives, which only seek discharge. The drive aims at acting; the compulsion to repeat deploys its force and manifests itself in the '*Agieren*' of the transference. Meaning has to be constructed; representation is no longer a given, but the result of work. The unconscious has to be constituted. Furthermore, the drive gives the object its full importance. André Green (2002) makes the hypothesis that to establish itself, representation needs the participation of the object; the figuration of the latter amalgamates with a mode of representation resulting from the exigencies of the body. It is from this conjunction that the unconscious is truly born (p. 69). The second topography is thus linked up with the first. Consequently, force and meaning are mediatised by representation: representation as delegation of the exigencies of the body in search of satisfaction, and thus of the object; representation of satisfaction involving the object; and representation of the demands addressed to the object becoming a demand to signify the demand (p. 69). These very concise formulations bring the drive-based body and the object, as well as access to representation, into a dialectical relationship. André Green's thinking stems from clinical work with non-neurotic psychic organisations where difficulties of thinking are in the foreground. It was Bion who opened up this domain of research. This clinical thinking renews, does it not, the conceptions of the unconscious and preconscious alike? The deficiencies of the preconscious (which characterise, in particular, the 'operational thinking' *[pensée opératoire]* described by the Paris Psychosomatic School and, in particular, Pierre Marty) make it possible to grasp the relations between perception and representation and may justify the modifications of the classical analytic setting (face-to-face situation rather than the lying position on the couch).

Furthermore, when the unconscious becomes an attribute, there is a real risk of the concept of the unconscious being watered down or dissolved. Is this not what is implied by the unconscious to which the neurosciences refer? Is there, in fact, a continuity between the unconscious and the conscious or, on the contrary, a radical discontinuity?

In analytic practice, the method based on the analysand's free association and the analyst's free-floating attention is aimed, through the process of formal and topographical regression, at letting signs of unconscious representations and affects emerge. This implies that we cannot be satisfied with the description, or the visual and visual perception of a session by means of recordings and films. The 'raw' material must be thought through; in other words, it must pass through conscious *and* unconscious representations. Interpretation during the session originates from the work of transformation brought about by the analyst's thinking; it arises from that inner discourse of the analyst of which Jean-Claude Rolland has spoken, or from co-thinking, to use Daniel Widlöcher's term. Or again from Bion's dreaming thought. Thinking about clinical work implies a gap, a leap between theory and practice. Metapsychology is indispensable to us even if it is revisable, as Freud showed by moving from the first topography to the second. The countertransference has become the favoured instrument of the analyst for understanding the analysand's transference, which, by definition, is unconscious. This countertransference, whether understood in the classical sense or in the sense of projective identifications, is in any case also unconscious, and the 'meta' position, the position from above, so to speak, which allows for insight, can only come after the event. The analyst's unconscious is playing an increasingly important role in permitting and facilitating the psychic transformations necessary in analytic work. Bionian perspectives laid great stress on this aspect. The question of communication from unconscious to unconconscious outlined by Freud has thus returned today in other forms. The complex developments in Kleinian and post-Kleinian analysis on the different aspects of projective identification give greater depth to the unconscious dimension of thought-transferences *(Gedankenübertragungen)*. From quite a different perspective, Michel de M'Uzan has suggested that 'chimeras' are formed during the session, which stem from the encounter between the unconsciouses of the patient and the analyst.

Which unconscious? For which psychoanalysis? These are open questions! Freud's considerations on the unconscious ended in 1938 by acknowledging 'the profound obscurity of unconscious psychical life'. Psychoanalytic research is constantly trying to penetrate this unknown.

The problem of language

Today, more than 23 languages are spoken in Europe. The EPF has three official languages: English, French, and German. During congresses, the main communications are translated simultaneously into these three languages, which signifies that 20 or so languages are not translated! English is thus now the main language of communication. A sad fate, indeed, for the language of Shakespeare, which has lost a large part of its richness in the process!

In clinical exchanges, the encounter with analysts of varied horizons in different languages highlights the questions that we are constantly raising with regard to analytic thinking, language, and our means of exchange. The plays of language and the polysemy of words are often lost in translation and this no doubt contributes to favouring the case narrative to the detriment of the psychic movement of analysis. Jean Laplanche has made us particularly sensitive to the question of translation, not only from the language of one country to another but also from the language of a patient to our own; and also, within each one of us, the translation into words of a material (let's call it, with Freud, the drive representative) which requires a major work of transformation to put it into thought. We are constantly exerting ourselves, therefore, at these different levels of translation. We are always confronted with loss or the gain of translation, with the genius of each language, which reveals itself in the encounter with the foreigner. Interpretation in psychoanalysis confronts us with the value of words and their 'magic', a fact that Freud emphasised as early as 1890:

> Words are the most important media by which one man seeks to bring his influence to bear on another; words are a good method of producing mental changes in the one to whom they are addressed. (1890a, p. 292)

The words in question are those of the discourse; that is, of spoken language where the meaning is conveyed by tonality, by the inflections of the voice, by its own music, which transmits affects; the words of the analysand required by the fundamental rule, which itself is inflected by the transferential address; and finally, the words of the analyst born of evenly-suspended listening which deconstructs the narrative speech of the analysand and gives rise to a spoken or withheld interpretation. The citation from Freud already contains the principal ingredients of the process, with the emphasis placed on language and the influence of one person on another through the discourse.

Our international meetings sensitise us through the experience of multiculturalism to certain dimensions of language and echo the questions that we meet with in the analytic situation. This is so even when we are in the context of just one language, for language conveys all the dimensions of culture. The EPF has been concerned with linguistic questions since the beginning. Raymond de Saussure, in his first editorial article for the *Information Bulletin of the EPF* in 1966, evoked the linguistic difficulties involved in scientific communication in Europe, where 20 or so languages are spoken. This has remained a constant concern and has led to the scientific study of the problems raised by multilinguism. Jacqueline Amati Mehler, Simona Argentieri and Jorge Canestri (1990) have proposed an elaboration of the main theoretical and clinical questions raised by the relationship to language that the analytic situation elucidates in cases of multilingualism and monolongualism alike. During his presidency, Alain Gibeault promoted studies as well as a symposium in 1998 on psychoanalysis and languages in Europe. These preoccupations of the EPF drew support from psychoanalytic contributions in different countries. Thus Jean Laplanche (1997), who concerned himself as early as 1957 with the problems of translating Freud, before undertaking in 1983 the translation of Freud's work into French *(Oeuvres complètes)*, extended the problem of translation by integrating it with an original conception of metapsychology.

Translation *(Übersetzung)* is the word that Freud uses, very early on in a letter to Fliess dated 6 December 1896 to designate the way the psychical apparatus is constituted and its differentiation into unconscious, preconscious, and conscious. He then proposes a theory of repression:

> A failure of translation – this is what is known clinically as 'repression'. The motive for it is always a release of the unpleasure that would be generated by translation; it is as though this unpleasure provokes a disturbance of thought that does not permit the work of translation. (Masson, 1985, p. 208)

In the introduction to his article 'The Unconscious' (Freud, 1915e), he asks the question:

> How are we to arrive at a knowledge of the unconscious? It is of course only as something conscious that we know it, after it has undergone transformation *(Umsetzung)* or translation *(Übersetzung)* into something conscious. Psychoanalytic work shows us every day that translation of every kind is possible. (p. 166)

The analytic situation induces a double translation: first, a translation of psychic states into language; and then their translation in the communication to the Other of the transference. The first consists in giving word-presentations to thing-presentations, words that then become an instrument for perceiving internal states. The other level of translation concerns what is said, and in what way, in the transferential address. To this movement of translation is opposed repression or the different modes of resistance against the pressure of conflictual infantile sexuality. We know how recourse to learned words or the words of another language can be used to attenuate too much libidinal or aggressive excitation. Latin, which was much more widely used in the past, had the double advantage of being a learned language and a dead language! Hence Freud speaks of *'matrem nudam'*; and, elsewhere, he reports Chroback's 'prescription' for a hysterical patient: *'Penis normalis dosim repetatur'!* It is not only sexuality that is diverted by foreign words but aggressivity also, along with murderous wishes. A French-speaking patient, evoking the term that he had fixed for his analysis, suddenly used the English word 'deadline'. In this way he was communicating to me the idea of death that this end signified, death given as much as death received. Claude Hagège (1985) writes: 'Languages differ not in respect of what they can or cannot express but in respect of what they oblige us to say or not say' (p. 62). In the word 'deadline', English obliges us to speak of death.

Jean Laplanche has given an important place to the theory of repression as translation by placing the accent on the idea of verbal or non-verbal 'enigmatic messages' transmitted by adults to the child without either of them being aware of it. Confronted with these messages, the child translates them as best he can with the language he has at his disposal. Infantile sexual theories are an affective, imaginative, and intellectual translation of the adult's message. Translation, in this sense, becomes the equivalent of construction. For Laplanche, the work of analysis is thus a work of deconstruction, of 'de-translation' obtained through interpretation. He opposes construction as re-construction of the past, a task shared between the analyst and the analysand, and self-construction, a new version of oneself, an operation carried out by the analysand alone. For Laplanche, interpretation/de-translation leaves the field free for a new translation: we undo the preconscious so that a new preconscious may reconquer what has been left to one side. This theory rests on the existence of representations; but can one still speak of translation when

93

we are dealing with drive impulses, that is, with representatives which may never have given rise to representations owing to denial or foreclosure *(Verleugnung or Verwerfung)*? Is one not faced, then, with the need for a work of transformation as can be achieved through sublimation?

The encounter with the foreigner in us or in the other arouses antagonistic impulses of attraction, but also of fear and rejection. Introjection and projection are primitive drive impulses. The work of culture *(Die Kulturarbeit)*, which humanises us, but which is also a work of sublimation, a work of 'taming the drives', is designed to help us encounter the other in his alterity and to accept the possibility of being partly transformed by this encounter.

I would like to say one more word on the implications of translation in this encounter with alterity. Many of us experience disappointment, frustration, and irritation when we are confronted with the difficulties and laborious efforts of our exchanges in foreign languages. There is, of course, the sense of betrayal of translation, but especially the experience of loss on the narcissistic and object level: the feeling of being amputated of a part of oneself, a feeling of painful castration. But there is also the sense of losing our identificatory references, the traces of our past love-objects conveyed by our mother language. And yet the entire process of symbolisation rests on the loss of a thing that the word represents in its absence. Words are thus always only equivalents that are capable of migrating from one language to another.

Do we feel nostalgia for a primal and basic language that would spare us all this work?! Are we constantly tempted by the illusory offer of a symbolism that would provide a simultaneous translation/interpretation, without remainder, without loss, and which would make understanding effortless (!), by an illusory wish for a key to dreams to which the psychoanalytic interpretation of dreams is opposed?

Under these conditions, how does this confrontation of languages enrich us? Beyond the wish to understand and to make ourselves understood, it seems to me that there is a gain from the translation that our European exchanges require of us. For me it lies in the psychic mobility, the capacities for linguistic inventions to which translation gives rise. This movement is also that which inspires us in the analytic encounter of two psyches in each other's presence. Finally, the passage from one language to another, from one culture to another, determines an area of play, and, strictly speaking, of representation.

Conclusion

The crisis of psychoanalysis today has its origin not only in the current state of the external world but also in a loss of confidence in psychoanalysis that is situated at an internal level and affects psychoanalysts themselves. We must strengthen our intimate conviction that there is a future for psychoanalysis by supporting the work of psychoanalysts. While many changes have occurred in recent years, the scientific objectives of the EPF remain essentially unchanged: more than ever, it is up to us to consolidate the identity of psychoanalysts and to promote psychoanalysis both as a science and a practice.

Translated from the French by Andrew Weller, Paris

References

AMATI MEHLER, J., ARGENTIERI, S., & CANESTRI, J. (1990). *La Babele dell'Inconscio*. Milan: Raffaelo Cortina. [(1994) *Le Babel de l'Inconscient*. Paris, PUF].

FREUD, S. (1890a). Psychical (or Mental) Treatment. *S.E. 7*, pp. 283–304.

FREUD, S. (1900). The Interpretation of Dreams. *S.E. 5*, pp. 4–5.

FREUD, S. (1915). 'The Unconscious'. *S.E. 14*, pp. 161–215.

FREUD, S. (1940 [1938]). An Outline of Psycho-Analysis. *S.E. 23*, pp. 141–207.

GREEN, A. (2002). *La pensée clinique*. Paris: Odile Jacob.

HAGÈGE, C. (1985). *L'homme de paroles. Contribution linguistique aux sciences humaines*. Paris: Arthème Fayard.

LAPLANCHE, J. (1997). *Le primat de l'Autre en psychanalyse* (studies from 1967 to 1992). Paris: Flammarion.

MASSON, J. M. (Ed.) (1985). *The Complete Letters of Sigmund Freud to Wilhelm Fliess 1887–1904*. Cambridge, MA: Belknap Press.

MOSCOVICI, M. (1990). *L'ombre de l'objet*. Paris: Seuil.

Encounters and Infallible Signs

Peter Wegner

I would like to begin by extending a special word of thanks to the current Executive and the President of the EPF, Serge Frisch, for offering me the welcome opportunity to share with you some of my thoughts and associations concerning my various activities in the EPF as they have developed over the years. As expressly requested, I am going to take this special opportunity to give an account of some of my experiences prior to and during my period of office of presidency viewed from a more personal perspective, and it is to that effect that the following account distinguishes itself from the final report I provided at the end of my term of office as EPF President 2008–2012 (Wegner, 2012).

As for some of my predecessors, nomination as a candidate for the office of President of the EPF came rather as a surprise to me and almost, I would say, accidentally – more than likely arising from the many previous personal encounters and conversations with different colleagues from the most varied European Societies. I truly think that without my increasing and ongoing interest in attending the different international conferences on offer, along with my extensive and diversified reading of psychoanalytic literature, both setting in immediately after the completion of my psychoanalytic training (1981–1986), I would never have received the chance of finally being made President-Elect on the Council in Spring 2007 in Barcelona.

Around the time of my training, the psychoanalytic institute of Tübingen/Stuttgart particularly distinguished itself through its active engagement in the DPV, the EPF and the IPA. Furthermore, the psychoanalytic lectures, regularly given by Prof. Wolfgang Loch (who held a professorship of psycho-analysis and psychotherapy at the university clinic of Tübingen over many years), offered an excellent and unique opportunity to learn a great deal about the developments of international psychoanalysis. And I believe that this was also one of the main reasons why many of the members of my institute – as far as it was possible for them for various reasons – at that time felt comfort-able in attending the international conferences on offer. As his successor Prof. Heinz Henseler was admitted to the Chair, so in his own way, he continued the tradition initiated and fostered by Wolfgang Loch. So, with the wisdom of hindsight, I now would say that back then a great many of us members felt hungry for learning more about the further developments of psychoanalysis and thus were keen to look beyond the edge of the plate of our own local psychoanalytic institute in order to extend our horizons and develop an ever broader perspective on psychoanalysis.

What in this regard afforded us a first and unique opportunity at that time, were the so-called conferences of the 'Psychoanalytic Associations of Central Europe' (with the majority of participants coming from Germany, Holland, Austria and Switzerland). The language spoken at those conferences was German and the conferences were specifically tailored to meet the needs and interests of the candidates. One of the first conferences I attended was the one in Bamberg in the year 1980 with the theme: 'The Return of War and Persecution in Psychoanalyses'. I recall that I was only 28 years old then, and had not yet been admitted to psychoanalytic training; therefore I had to first apply for special admission to be allowed to attend the conference in Bamberg. It was actually there, where – for the first time – I came face to face with the fact of what it means to know one's own history, but not yet having been able to process it in any substantial way (Henseler & Kuchen-buch, 1982). I was deeply moved and inwardly shaken by the things I learned from the different presentations at the conference in Bamberg as well as from the extremely personal contributions to the discussions. And it was this expe-rience that intensified my wish and strengthened my decision to undergo a personal psychoanalysis. The following year, in 1981, after being admitted to psychoanalytic training, I then was able to begin my training analysis.

But there was another encounter I would like to mention in this context, as it proved to be a paradigmatic experience, with an unforgettable and deci-sive influence upon my life. It was at the time, when I was still a candidate in psychoanalytic training, when Hillel Klein of Israel was a guest at our psychoanalytic institute in Tübingen in April 1983. It was the first time after the war that he had visited Germany, and I had been asked to be his personal tour guide and show him the cultural values of the city of Tübingen. It was on a warm spring afternoon and Hillel Klein and myself were strolling the streets watching the many people sitting in the pavement cafes enjoying the first warm spring sun. Hitherto, the both of us had solely been speaking English to each other. But, all of a sudden, Hillel Klein said to me in German: 'Germany has really changed. Now people are sitting outside in the street again. In the past they all used to be in hiding and seeking shelter in their houses.' Following that, I learned some more details about his family history, that is, about their persecution and deportation and the eventual escape to Israel. The both of us were profoundly touched. He subsequently changed his mind on reading his paper at the institute, as he had originally intended, in English. When delivering his lecture, he spontaneously transformed the English manuscript into German. I believe it can truly be said, that for all of us in the institute it was a deeply moving experience to hear him being able to speak his mother tongue 'again'.

But there were many more surprises in store for me, when in the following years I began to increasingly frequently attend the various international psychoanalytic conferences. However, there was one considerable difficulty, which arose from the barrier of foreign languages. Many of us had problems with the English language (not to mention French or Spanish), and the simultaneous translations often stumbled over the complexity and elaborateness of the psychoanalytic formulations. So very often, one could consider oneself lucky to get even some vague idea of what was being discussed in the papers presented. This could be very frustrating and it was a real challenge not to give up and to give it another try next time.

But there was another particular problem to come to terms with: we were surprised to learn that our teachers and colleagues, who at their local institute appeared very eloquent and self-confident, were conspicuously absent on the international stage. As I understand it, one of the reasons for this could be seen as originating from the fact that, because of the forced migration of psychoanalysis from Germany during the Nazi era, psychoanalysis in Germany was prevented from keeping up with the latest international developments of our discipline, as a corollary of which a great scientific backlog emerged. But, apart from this, we also had a difficult and hard time on the international stage, because of having to come to terms with our role of being German after the Holocaust. Of course, it is difficult to find the right words to broach this subject, and I think to do so would take more space than I have here. But I should still like to take this opportunity of clarifying, that on the one side, and overall, we were given a friendly reception but, on the other side, we were also faced with a rather covertly sceptical, doubtful and rejecting attitude. Together with our own guilt-ridden uncertainty around how to deal with our German past, this produced a rather difficult situation. Thus, notwithstanding the content-related stimuli and inspirations, the personal encounters and ensuing friendships from which we strongly benefited, this was a situation that demanded of us a partly unconscious and, in any event, challenging working through. Over the years I came to realise that many of us felt no longer prepared to expose themselves to this challenging and irritating dilemma and eventually gave up and withdrew from the international stage altogether, a situation I personally always deeply regretted. Although it was not always easy for me either and there were some irrational fears involved to be dealt with, I decided to not let myself be deterred by it.

Now, there is another early experience in my professional career that deserves special mention here: the founding of a small clinical group of candidates from different countries (Argentina, Australia, England, Denmark, Finland, Italy, Canada, Peru, USA and Germany), which met on a regular basis as part of the IPSO pre-conferences of the IPA congress, where the participants were given the opportunity to discuss their own clinical experiences (Madrid, 1983; Hamburg, 1985; Montreal, 1987; Rome, 1989).

This subsequently led to my participation in the organisation of the IPSO conference in Hamburg in 1985. In spite of enormous fears over my lack of knowledge of the English language, I managed to give, for the first time, a short presentation in English. The ensuing personal relationships made it much easier for me to attend the conferences from now on, because I always met one or other colleagues that I already knew and with whom I could spent the midday breaks or the evenings. As the participants over the years inevitably evolved into different directions, the clinical group finally dissolved. I must also mention here the pre-history of this, the first IPA congress on German soil after the Holocaust. The decision was made not to choose Berlin as its venue (see among others Anne-Marie Sandler in Hermanns, 2015, pp. 264). It was only at the second attempt that the choice fell on Hamburg (1985). Understandably, we all were very much affected by this and it confirmed and intensified the above-mentioned feelings of uncertainty on our part. In the meantime I attended the 'Weekend Conferences' in London. This gave me the valuable opportunity to regularly discuss my clinical work with Mervin Glasser.

Since 1989 (Heidelberg), I myself was able to attend all of the annual EPF conferences with the exception of only two (Nice, 1995 and Helsinki, 2004). With a heart full of enthusiasm, I immediately, after completing my psychoanalytic training and qualifying as a psychoanalyst, had registered for an EPF seminar for associate members. The seminar was held in Prague in 1992, and it was the tenth time that such a seminar had taken place as part of the EPF programme. I was impressed by the openness of the working atmosphere and how easy it was to follow the clinical presentations of the colleagues from the different countries. On this occasion I was fortunate to once again meet Nicolass Treurniet (who was one of the four supervisors, together with Alain Gibeault, Thalia Vergopoulo and Anette Watillon). Then and there, I had the wonderful opportunity of gaining an even better idea of Nicolass Treurniet's outstanding psychoanalytic clinical skills. This was also the beginning of a long-standing friendship with him, which, above all, gave me the necessary confidence to not give up in my efforts to establish contacts with colleagues outside Germany (see Legueltel & Wegner, 1993). Furthermore, thanks to the initiative of another participant of this seminar, Rob Wille from Holland, a small group of European colleagues (from Belgium, England, France, Holland, Italy and Germany) spontaneously got together and decided to meet from then on once a year (1993–1998) for an extended weekend in order to discuss their clinical work. The intense clinical discussions in this group, together with the opportunity of getting to know each other on a more personal level, were a first step in the direction of dealing with my poor knowledge of the English language, in a much more anxiety-free manner. But perhaps more importantly, the intensive group work, in particular, helped me to develop a clearer and more concrete idea of what the deficits and challenges in psychoanalytic training in Germany had been facing, and, by contrast, how many developments, with the potential to improve psychoanalytic work, had taken place over the last twenty years elsewhere in Europe. To all intents and purposes, this proved to be a very clarifying and liberating experience for me.

It was a special honour for me when, on occasion of his 70th birthday, I

101

was invited by Nick Treurniet in 1996 to attend a symposium in Amsterdam. Besides the fact that I, on this particular occasion, was given the chance to come to know the other presenters while listening to, and participating in, the many intense discussions (among others Charles M. T. Hanly, Anton O. Kris, Han Groen-Prakken and Duveken Engels), I took the opportunity to present *ex ante* – on a trial basis, that is – my paper for the acquisition of full membership in the DPV (Wegner, 1996; 2000).

When I was eventually appointed Chairman of the Guest Committee (1988–1992) of the Tübingen/Stuttgart Institute, this proved another useful and enriching experience in terms of making international contacts. In those days we almost exclusively invited English-speaking psychoanalysts to present their papers at our institute. As a result, over the years, a network of close ties and friendships with analysts from abroad developed. Back then we were not yet able to benefit from the advantages of being linked by email, and our institute was not even equipped with a fax machine. During my term of office as Chair of the Guest Committee, the following psychoanalysts were invited to Tübingen: Nick Treurniet, Jaqueline Amati-Mehler, Terttu Eskelinen de Folch, Ron Baker, Betty Joseph, Janine Chasseguet-Smirgel, Jaques Berna, Ilany Kogan, Adam Limentani, Andre Haynal, Evelyne Albrecht Schwaber, Mervin Glasser, Elisbeth Bott Spillius, Patrick Casement, and last but not least Christopher Bollas. All of these personal encounters were very stimulating and inspiring for me and tremendously broadened both my professional and personal perspectives. But also, and above all, these personal encounters with psychoanalysts from other psychoanalytic cultures and traditions helped me develop a self-critical stance and dare to put my own firm beliefs into question.

For the period 1996–1997, Ekkehard Gattig (then President of the DPV) and for the period 1998–1999 his successor, Winfried Trimborn, appointed me a member of the programme committee of the DPV autumn conferences. This proved an excellent opportunity to learn a great deal about how big conferences work and how the format of such an event must be designed in order to launch a discussion in a large group (600 to 800 participants). I particularly remember well the autumn conference in Wiesbaden in 1997. Its theme was: 'Thinking in the Presence of the Other' with impressive main presentations by Roy Schafer, Owen Renik and David Tuckett, followed by very lively and controversial discussions.

Furthermore, I profited immensely from seven clinical-theoretical seminars with Christopher Bollas. Together with Eva Schmid-Gloor and other colleagues from Tübingen, Zurich and Geneva, I organised those seminars (2000–2006), each one held on a long weekend, alternately in Tübingen and Zurich, where we had the opportunity to gather in a small group and present and discuss clinical cases, as well as to consider different theoretical issues. What appealed to me most was when Christopher Bollas developed and discussed his own ideas concerning 'Free Association and the Transference', which about two years later were published in a small volume (Bollas, 2002).

There was yet another significant event, which I came across in the form of an invitation to a conference in the year 2000, which I received from Laura Tognoli and Gabriele Pasquali from Genova. My participation in this conference prepared me well for my future activities and my work in the EPF. At that time, Gabriele and I already knew each other from sharing a particular experience, which made such a deep impression on me that it has remained in my memory up until the present day. At the IPA congress in Buenos Aires in 1991, we both were given a similar task: each of us was asked to draft a written report of one of the panels to subsequently be submitted to the Chairman of the programme committee, Harold P. Blum. Faced with this challenging task, I spend an agonising few hours working through the night, finally, at around three o'clock in the morning, taking a walk to Harold P. Blum's hotel and pushing under the door of his hotel room my hand-written scribblings. It was presumably a similarly particular experience for Gabriele as it was for me, because later we both assured each other of how exciting the whole enterprise had been.

Incidentally, the panel on which I wrote the report, was chaired by Betty Joseph, whom I met personally for the first time in 1991, and who some time later I had the chance to invite to Tübingen to give a presentation at our local institute. Now, to cut a long story short, Laura and Gabriele invited me and my wife, the psychoanalyst Christine Wegner, to participate in the EPF-NAPsaC conference in Camoglie (Italy), which they were organising at the time and which was to be held in 2000. In the course of this exclusively clinical seminar we had, for the very first time, the opportunity to become more familiar with the psychoanalytic work of some of our American colleagues. We then had also the pleasure of attending the next EPF-NAPsaC seminar in Lugano (2002), on which occasion we were asked by Laura, Gabriele and Edward Nersessian from New York, if we wanted to organise the next EPF-

NAPsaC seminar for 2004 in Tübingen. We were fully aware of the honour of hosting such an international meeting for the first time in Germany and thus spontaneously accepted.

The seminar held in Tübingen in 2004 proved to be a very moving experience. Altogether there were 33 participants from America and 33 participants from Europe. All of the psychoanalysts worked in mixed small clinical groups (North America/Europe) and presented clinical cases. Among the participants were: Helen and Donald Meyers, Howard Levine, Edward Nersessian, Robert Pyles, the Margolis, Mary K. O'Neil Lowy and Gail S. Reed from North America, as well as Elfriede Fidal, Evelyne Sechaud (who since April 2004 had been elected President of the EPF), Liliane Abensour, Viviane Chetrit-Vatine, Stephen Grosz, Yolanda Gampel, Patrick Miller, Marilia Aisenstein and Rifka Eifermann from Europe. In one of the sessions there was a Jewish colleague from the US, who presented a clinical case. She was so churned up inside because of being in Germany for the first time since the war, that we spontaneously decided to discontinue the case presentation and instead to talk about her personal life and fate. Thanks to the active engagement and participation of our colleagues from Tübingen we then were able to offer all of the guests an invitation for dinner in one of the private households. Finally, on the next evening, there was a festive dinner at the Bebenhausen Monastery including an unforgettable concert of the Ensemble L'Ornamento, which in the years to come won a number of prizes and achieved a certain amount of acclaim.

We were so pleased with the course of the conference that we (Laura, Gabriele and myself) hit upon the idea of also offering to our candidates the possibility to gain first experiences in terms of international exchange. We also managed to persuade Jutta Gutwinski-Jeggle of the benefits of this idea. Consequently, we were able to organise clinical seminars for our candidates over a period of four years, which took place in Tübingen and in Genoa. Half of the participants in the small clinical groups were candidates from Tübingen, and half of them were from Genoa. All of the candidates presented a training case, each one of them supervised by a teaching analyst of the other institute.

Shortly afterwards I received a phone call from Evelyne Sechaud and, all of a sudden, found myself in the situation of having to decide whether to accept or not – at short notice – the vacant position of General Secretary of the EPF. After lengthy consideration, I came to the conclusion that it would be neither feasible nor advisable to alter, at short notice, the long term schedule for my patients' sessions and therefore, much to my regret, I had to decline. But Evelyne was persistent in her wish to offer me when the time came – at not such short notice – the candidacy for the office of EPF Vice-President. Full of delight and with my heart pounding, I accepted. At the Council meeting in February 2005 in Belgrade, I was elected EPF Vice-President. This was the beginning of a new chapter in my life.

Whilst looking at the background factors that eventually led to my being elected President of the EPF in 2007, I couldn't help querying in my mind how I made it to this position at all. For sure, I've always had a keen interest in meeting other psychoanalysts personally. The reading and reception of the different psychoanalytic texts is usually much easier for me if I know the author in person. But beyond this, by illuminating some of the background circumstances of my professional career and my personal life I also wanted to illustrate that it is, to this present day, by no means a matter of course for a German psychoanalyst after the Holocaust to be invested with an office in the psychoanalytic community. Of course, I was helped by the fact that before me, other German psychoanalysts had occupied various offices in the EPF: Samir Stephanos was a member of the Editor Board of the *Bulletin* (1972–1977), Gemma Jappe was General Secretary (1980–1984), Heinz Henseler was Vice-President (1984–1988), and Gabriele Junkers was the Editor of the *Bulletin* (1996–2000) as well as General Secretary (2000–2004). Nevertheless, when measured by the fact that the DPV has since become the largest member organisation of the EPF, this seems to be a significant under-representation. Incidentally, the EPF owes the new layout and the current unique form of the *Bulletin*, 'Psychoanalysis in Europe' (beginning with *Bulletin* 47 in autumn 1996), published in German, English and French simultaneously, to Gabriele Junkers. Each year anew I eagerly await its publication.

How can one explain the fact that there were only a relatively small number of German colleagues who were willing to actively participate in the EPF? As already referred to, the upheavals caused by the Nazi past and the forced emigration of psychoanalysis from Germany had a direct and significant impact on psychoanalysis in Germany. But I think that at this point it is fair to make it very clear that there is probably another substantial reason. After the Second World War, psychoanalysis in Germany rapidly developed, particularly under the influence of important events and profound changes in the late 1960s, in the wave of the students' revolt of 1968. As it was the student movement's mission to commit to social issues, simultaneously adopting a heretic stance of 'emancipatory' and 'anti-authoritarian' ideas, which could best be formulated by connecting the findings of psychoanalysis with revolutionary practice, this resulted in a radical criticism of the 'prudish' and 'hypocritical' sexual morality of previous generations, which additionally found ideological support from some of the most innovative and progressive thinkers of the 'Frankfurt School'. And this, I would surmise, is also part of the explanation why during the second half of the 20th century, the publications of so many international psychoanalysts were translated into German. It can therefore be said that up to a certain point in time there had been no shortage of international psychoanalytic literature translated into German. Notwithstanding, it took a rather long time until, along with the theoretical perspective of international psychoanalysis, the clinical psychoanalytic experience was integrated into psychoanalytic training in Germany in an effective manner. For instance, as I experienced myself during my own psychoanalytic training, there were some teachers who were still very reluctant to accept and clinically work with the concept of counter-transference. So, one could say, that for a very long time, German psychoanalysis failed to keep pace with the developments of international psychoanalysis. And I am afraid, in many respects, this continues to be the case today. This is, of course, a humiliating fact, which, more or less consciously or unconsciously, is still weighing heavily on many of us and which has considerable and disturbing consequences. For all that, it was the favourable atmosphere of my training institute that persuaded me to direct my gaze, as often as possible, towards the psychoanalytic world 'outside'. The urge for discovery, the open-mindedness, the tolerance of not-knowing and the readiness and capacity of listening without purpose and intent – all these are valuable dispositions that at some stage in the course of your professional path either come by you in an entirely individual way, or else pass you by forever.

During my term of office as Vice-President under the presidency of Evelyne Sechaud I quickly learned how the EPF works. Evelyne was a superb president, from whom I have learned a great deal and whom I still deeply appreciate today. The IPA and the EPF fulfil two very different functions and serve different tasks. The EPF (as a federation of Societies and not of individual members) has set itself the task of furthering the exchange between the different European Societies and of supporting their training efforts. In all this the EPF has to make do without any administrative authority, as this status is not conferred to it by the constitution and bylaws. Of course, this 'abstinence', as far as scientific, political or professional political issues are concerned, has always led to controversial discussions. It is mainly due to the active initiative of the French Psychoanalytical Society, but equally to that of the Swiss Psychoanalytical Society, that from the founding of the EPF the course was set to this effect (Groen-Prakken, 1986; Lebovici, 1986, etc.).

A distinctive feature of the EPF (contrary to that of the federations in North and South America: NAPsaC and FEPAL) is the fact that in Europe we have an enormous diversity of languages and cultures. I have already mentioned the EPF *Bulletin*, which is quite exceptional and unique in its form, because it is the only psychoanalytic medium of publication to be edited in three languages simultaneously (German, English and French), now for some decades. This, of course, requires a great deal of work, time-consuming coordination and numerous dedicated and committed translators. This alone has made the EPF *Bulletin* an important organ in fulfilling an integrative task: the development of European psychoanalysis in the second half of the 20th century. What it means to translate complex and highly differentiated psychoanalytic texts is generally not valued enough. I am sure that the translators who undertake this challenging task with great passion and commitment would have plenty to say about it. In Europe in particular there are numerous cultural and linguistic differences, school-specific (psychoanalytic) interpretations and historically evolved peculiarities, so that the seemingly simple task of translating a text from one language into another, more often than not actually proves to be an enormous challenge. This particularly applies to German psychoanalytic texts since 1945, which have been very rarely translated into English, French or Spanish. The academic-scientific style of the writing would anyhow have been difficult to translate; and besides, those texts, over a long period of time, have not really developed in such a clinically substantial way as to make an enriching and meaningful contribution to other psychoanalytic traditions outside Germany. But, nevertheless, the ongoing commitment and ever-renewed efforts in this area give rise to hopes that changes may come about slowly.

I was aware of all this when I started my term of office as the first German EPF President at the end of the Vienna Annual Conference in 2008, and I therefore had a great deal of respect for the challenging tasks and varied du-

107

ties that lay ahead of me. I consider it a particularly fortunate coincidence that the newly elected Executive harmonised in the most effective and best possible way. Almost from the first instance, we managed to develop an unusual degree of team spirit that went beyond all cultural difference. Without this enduring spirit of cooperation, we would not have been so effective and successful in coping with the ever-increasing number of tasks. I really do feel profoundly indebted to Ronny Jaffè (Vice-President), Jonathan Sklar (Vice-President), Denny Panitz (General Secretary), Anne Rosenberg (Treasurer) and Dieter Bürgin (General Editor). I can truly say that we all managed to quickly develop a positive working atmosphere and thus solve the problems and tasks ahead of us in the best interest of the EPF. Of course, there were other times too, when we felt strained and exhausted, or when we had to withstand conflicts and to deal with controversies. But apart from that, in the end, we succeeded in sustaining an overall amicable and personal atmosphere. On top of that, I can also say with a certain degree of joy and personal satisfaction that the majority of the presidents in the Council supported and actively encouraged us in our work in the most collegial, even friendly manner.

But still I would like to mention an utterly striking, but singular event that occurred at one point during my presidency as I approached the end of my term in office, when my German origins caught up with me at last. And – let me say it right away – it deeply hurt me. Now, it is part of the duties and responsibilities of the President and the Executive to organise and chair the EPF Council meetings, which take place twice a year. At those meetings all of the presidents of the European member Societies also assemble in order to discuss all the unsolved tasks and come to a general agreement on the most important questions on the agenda. As the election periods of the different European Societies do not usually coincide, it sometimes happens that a new president attends the Council meeting for the very first time, or else it may happen that a president whose term of office will soon expire, will rise after his last session and say a few words of farewell. But sometimes the colleague concerned will speak his parting words only later during the joint dinner. That was the case in my second to last Council meeting in The Hague, in the autumn of 2011. Sometime between the main course and the dessert, one of our colleagues suddenly stood up and expressed his gratitude for the excellent cooperation, emphasising what he had personally gained from his valuable experiences as a member of the Council. And then – without prior notice or warning – he said: 'I might add, with Freud: "'I can heartily recommend the Gestapo to anyone."' This caused an immediate outburst of laughter at all the tables around me, whereas I myself turned deadly pale and fell silent. Nothing else happened. The colleague in question sat back down and the hubbub of voices at the tables rose again as if nothing had happened.

What was I supposed to do? Did I understand this correctly? Was this supposed to be a more or less undisguised critical comment concerning the President of the EPF? The Freud quotation is from the year 1938. The Nazi invasion of Austria that took place on 11 March was 'the signal for Freud's and his family's leaving' Vienna, although Freud until the last 'was reluctant' (Jones, 1957, p. 233). Finally, with the help of Jones and, even more so, of Marie Bonaparte, some members of Freud's family got permission to travel to England and 'on June 4, armed with all the necessary documents and exit permits, Freud, with his wife and daughter, took a final leave of the city, where he had dwelt for seventy-nine years and to which he had felt so bound' (p. 242). Jones continues:

> Freud retained his ironic attitude towards the complicated formalities that had to be gone through. One of the conditions for being granted an exit visum was that he sign a document that ran as follows: 'I, Prof. Freud, hereby confirm that after the Anschluss of Austria to the German Reich I have been treated by the German authorities and particularly the Gestapo with all the respect and consideration due to my scientific reputation, that I could live and work in full freedom, that I could continue to pursue my activities in every way I desired, that I found full support from all concerned in this respect, and that I have not the slightest reason for any complaints.' When the Nazi Commissar brought it along Freud had of course no compunction in signing it, but he asked if he might be allowed to add a sentence, which was: 'I can heartily recommend the Gestapo to anyone.' (p. 241)

Why the colleague chose this specific quotation, and what was the irony behind this with respect to the Council of the EPF could never really be uncovered. Maybe this is an example of the impact of the unconscious, which is, as we all know, something that can suddenly command us in the most drastic and radical way. In any case, the Council meeting continued and then ended on a routine basis, and it was not until afterwards that an intensive email exchange followed, along with many telephone calls with the different Executive members and with some of my German colleagues, more or less circling around the pressing question how to adequately deal with such a faux pas. Be that as it may, when I, on that specific evening at the dinner table, had the experience of suddenly not being able to respond, I knew that eventually at some point or other, 'general history' catches up with us as does our own 'personal history', irrespective of the fact that we, personally, cannot be held responsible for it. But still, what stays with us is a permanent sense of responsibility that can't ever be repudiated!

After all, it should not be forgotten that psychoanalytic working environments are by no means free of political interests, manipulations and power, political motives and strategies, and that also, more often than not, these remain undetected, while at the same time, silently exerting a destructive influence upon the commonly agreed upon objectives of psychoanalysis. Manuela Utrilla Robles, who, during one of my terms of office in the EPF, was in her role as European Representative of the IPA and as President of the Madrid Psychoanalytical Association a member of the Council, has written a very insightful and thought-provoking book on this specific topic (Utrilla Robles, 2013). Presently, scientific-political as well as professional-political conflicts are still underestimated, and I fear they will, if not dealt with adequately, be constantly on the increase, not merely within the different psychoanalytical societies and the IPA, but also within the EPF. Recent experience gained since the term of office of Evelyne Sechaud, who sought to deepen and intensify contacts with FEPAL, NAPsaC/APsaA and the IPA, seem to support and confirm the above-mentioned hypothesis in regard to South and North America. The intensive and continual consultations with FEPAL (Mariam Alizade, Enrique Nunez Jasso, and Leopold Nosek) and NAPsaC/APsaA (Harriet Basseches, Lynne Moritz, Warren Procci, Robert Pyles and Prudi Gourguechon) clearly contributed to continuing to develop collaboration with the other regions in a positive atmosphere of mutual understanding. However, as I see it, despite all the care taken and our greatest efforts, the basically unresolved question remains of whether and how the relationship between the IPA (as an international member organisation) and the three regional organisations (as federations of Societies) can be improved from an institutional point of view.

As a closing remark, I would like to emphasise that I personally was always committed to supporting adherence to the high frequency treatment method – and here I include the three sessions per week standard technique of the French training model. It is a pity that this specific detail (of the French training model) is often alleged as pretext and hence does, in fact, lead some analysts to believe that they can now justify requiring a lower treatment frequency for the Eitingon training model too, which is, for a number of reasons, not appropriate. But this is a theme in itself, which would afford a more extended and detailed discussion. Today we know that psychoanalytic work can be successfully done in a variety of settings, but we also know that an important and indispensable precondition for this is sufficient clinical experience with high frequency treatments. As I strongly believe that there will be in the future no better treatment method for many of our patients than psychoanalysis in the stricter sense, it was one of my main concerns during my period of office, both within the scope of the smaller conferences as well as the annual EPF conferences (Brussels, London, Copenhagen and Paris), to foster and to also, as much as possible, help further develop this basic clinical competency of contemporary psychoanalysis.

Translated from the German by M. A. Luitgard Feiks
and Jürgen Muck, Nürtingen am Neckar

References

BOLLAS, C. (2002). *Free Association. Ideas in Psychoanalysis.* Duxford, Cambridge: Icon Books Ltd.

GROEN-PRAKKEN, H. (1986). A European organization for psychoanalysis – why, how and when? In *Psychoanalysis in Europe. EPF Bulletin 26*, 11–68.

HENSELER, H., & KUCHENBUCH, A. (Eds.) (1982). *Die Wiederkehr von Krieg und Verfolgung in Psychoanalysen. Eine Sammlung der auf der Arbeitstagung der Mitteleuropäischen Psychoanalytischen Vereinigungen in Bamberg vom 30. März bis zum 3. April 1980 gehaltenen Referate sowie rückblickender Kommentare.* Private papers, Ulm-Berlin.

JONES, E. (1957). *Sigmund Freud. Life and Work, Volume Three: The Last Phase 1919–1939.* London: Hogarth Press.

LEBOVICI, S. (1986). Some recollections of the founding of EPF. *Psychoanalysis in Europe. EPF Bulletin 26*, 73–78.

LEGUELTEL, C., & WEGNER, P. (1993). Report on the 10th EPF Seminar for Associative Members, 1992. *Psychoanalysis in Europe. EPF Bulletin 40*(1), 72–74.

SANDLER, A.-M. (2015). Anne-Marie Sandler. In L. M. Hermanns (Ed.), *Psychoanalyse in Selbstdarstellungen. Band X*. Frankfurt/M.: Brandes & Apsel.

UTRILLA ROBLES, M. (2013). *Fanaticism in Psychoanalysis. Upheavals in the Institutions*. London. Karnac.

WEGNER, P. (1996). Passion, counter-transference enactment and breakdown in the psychoanalysis of a young woman. In H. Groen-Prakken (Ed.) (1996), *Psychoanalysis in a Post-Classical Context* (pp. 40–50). Assen: Van Gorcum.

WEGNER, P. (2000). Passion, counter-transference enactment and breakdown in the psychoanalysis of a young woman. *J. American Psychoanal. Assoc. 48*(3), 811–838.

WEGNER, P. (2012). Report from the EPF President 2008–2012. *Psychoanalysis in Europe. Bulletin 66*, 213–220.

The Future of Psychoanalysis is Built Today

Serge Frisch

Psychoanalysis, a great discovery, remains an extraordinary adventure and has been kept alive due to both the active commitment of all psychoanalysts and to organisations such as the European Psychoanalytical Federation. In contemporary society, thinking tends to be played down somewhat, with action taking precedence over reflection; the psychoanalytic approach, with its focus on reflection, is therefore an important resource for many distressed people. Therapies focusing on symptoms mirror present day society. However in the end, the therapeutic results of these therapies may turn out to be unsatisfactory because psychical reality is neither taken into account nor the 'discontents' in civilisation that are as much a factor today as they were when Freud first wrote of them.

We think of psychoanalysis as an intra- and inter-psychical approach, although other analysts might define psychoanalysis differently. These differences are indeed a rich source of potential developments. Psychoanalysis is concerned with situations in which the unconscious 'emerges' and has to face up to the challenge of treating extremely difficult patients and situations; but to meet that challenge, it is essential that our thinking remains truly psychoanalytic.

Europe has many distinguishing features – its history, its cultural diversity, its many languages – which, it must not be forgotten, have shaped psychoanalysis as we know it today. Paradoxically, that very diversity also represents the unity of Europe; it is an asset that can assist the EPF to go on developing the instrument that is psychoanalysis and thus further our learning. The presence of more than forty member societies in the Council of the EPF creates a special and unique forum for sharing our ideas and debating them. The three languages of the EPF – English, German and French – testify to the polysemy of European psychoanalysis and retaining them by our federation underscores their great symbolic value.

The presidents representing their Societies on the Council are the individuals best informed about the debates and, at times, reorientations that psychoanalysis experiences in their respective countries or, even more, the new interests and research fields of their members. They are also abreast of social and political changes that psychoanalysis may be exposed to in their countries. Thanks to all these presidents, the EPF maintains a tertiary position and enjoys a macroscopic view of the differing situations of psychoanalysis in Europe. It can thus encourage new ideas and scientific projects across the entire psychoanalytic community, which individual members of the different member Societies take advantage of.

The EPF represents a blend of cultures, a hallmark of Europe, and it must remain open to otherness even if in certain circumstances it is necessary to strive for mutual agreement and remain tolerant of any differences of opinion that exist in such rich and diverse cultures. Psychoanalysts do need authentic, stimulating and sometimes passionate debates; otherwise, psychoanalysis risks becoming commonplace and disappearing. The institutional practice of psychoanalysis requires both democracy and the need to take into account the requirements of our particular field.

My Executive shared the decision to call even more forcefully upon this rich European legacy of ours and to make the EPF more influential than it is at present in our ever-changing world of institutions.

Of course the EPF must remain true to the spirit of the scientific conception that its founding fathers laid down in 1969:

> The main aim of the EPF, as agreed at the foundation of the European Federation, was, in short, to maintain and promote Sigmund Freud's psychoanalysis. As this involved objectives of a decidedly non-political and non-legislative nature, by contrast with those of the IPA, it was decided that the EPF would serve as a forum for the mutual scientific exchange of Europe's psychoanalysts. (EPF webpage)

But given the institutional and administrative responsibilities of the EPF, as well as the issues of general and scientific policy that it must address, it is obvious that this objective has for some time now been shown to be insufficient. Although the present development of the EPF requires us to go beyond that initial aim, I would argue that it must not, all the same, be forgotten.

After World War II, analysis was completely devastated all over Europe with the exception of Great Britain and maybe the Netherlands and Sweden. Beside these few European countries the main headquarter of psychoanalysis was located in North America. One could say that in the early 1950s, analysis didn't yet exist in Latin America.

Today the situation is completely different. Fifty per cent of IPA analysts belong to the European region, to EPF member societies, while analysis is more or less starving in North America. In Latin America, psychoanalysis is still developing in a chaotic manner.

Today the strength and lively forces of psychoanalysis are clearly located in Europe. Europe is also the region producing the most theoretical contributions to psychoanalysis and we certainly can link the European development of psychoanalysis with the persisting European interest in analytic theory.

But, nevertheless, despite positive signs over these last years, we observe that over the past two or three decades, psychoanalysis has been confronted with a decline in the number of patients on the couch and a decrease in candidates in training. At the same time, fewer analysts hold teaching positions or positions of responsibility in hospitals.

To face these changes in the place of psychoanalysis in contemporary society, at the start of the new century the EPF implemented significant changes: the biannual congress became annual and the working parties were created in the frame of a new scientific policy. You will find details of these changes and the reorientations underlying them in the pieces of the then-presidents, David Tuckett and Evelyne Sechaud.

When my Executive assumed its functions, we were convinced that we too necessarily had to proceed with new adjustments of the very structure of the EPF in order to adapt the Federation to today's challenges. In effect, the amount of work that the Executive has to accomplish has grown considerably over time, now that there are more than forty societies represented on the Council. European issues have become more and more complex; on an international level, in our contacts with North and Latin America, differences of opinion are becoming more pronounced and the situation with the IPA is at times tense. It is therefore absolutely essential that the Executive be fully functional, with its members, each with his or her own contribution to make, working as a team in a spirit of collaboration and cohesion.

Whereas previously the six members of the Executive were elected at different times, the statutes now make it possible to elect a coherent team that remains in place for four years. With any institution, there exists a danger of becoming more and more administrative in outlook, thus leading to paralysis. But the EPF, intending clearly to be more effective, has had to hire a professional assistant-secretary to the Executive. This clearly will favour more flexibility and quicker adaptation to new situations.

But since we assumed our functions, the principal changes in our team have been centred on the scientific dimensions. As a space for clinical and theoretical debates, the EPF is a locus for research. The EPF's existence and future depend on the capacity of analysts to question and above all deepen the specificity of their practice and thought – a background that orients all of its scientific policy.

For its scientific projects, the EPF must take into account the diversity of the research models and the interrelation of the theoretical conceptions and clinical practices, but likewise the training models that exist in the European analytic community – that is, the Eitingon model and French model – an internal coherence of which each of us possesses. Having them interact with each other in order to understand their consequences on the future of the next generation of analysts seemed fundamental to us.

We've redirected the EPF's scientific orientation. If at the beginning of the century, the working parties were designed to define, say, the proper way to work, which implies a normative conception, we thought on the contrary that it was important to make the models and analytic notions dialogue with each other. The idea is to better understand the reasons and origins of the differences that exist between the analytic cultures of our European psychoanalytic societies. These differing conceptions might find their origins in the divergent readings of Freud's fundamental texts, in which language is doubtless influential. Yet a country's culture may through the years also influence how psychoanalysis is practiced. When psychoanalysis falls within a system of medical care, psychoanalysts are subject to the constraints of this system and likewise to the medical system's 'healthcare' philosophy. Psychoanalysis will develop differently than in a country where it does not have to adapt itself to the constraints of 'healthcare'. But it's also interesting to think about the consequences for psychoanalysis when these constraints do not exist.

As we've emphasised, the EPF's strength resides in the diversity of psychoanalytic clinical practice. Making these diverse clinical practices confront each other, making them dialogue with each other, debating their differences and the consequences that stem from them, flushing out preconceptions or shedding light on blind spots should be even further encouraged. The idea is not to suppress differences but to assume them and then understand them, to explore them and not to try to turn psychoanalysis into a politically correct theory by wearing away their differences. We remain convinced that it is essential to understand the origins of these differences and their consequences. For this reason we have promoted the creation of working groups (ad hoc groups, forums or working parties) by giving them an institutional framework in order to frame them in the least constraining way possible.

The main idea is thus to have analysts from European societies increasingly speak to each other. The consequences of these changes are interesting: group work among peers without a pre-established hierarchy greatly changes the work atmosphere. Each psychoanalyst is requested to lend his or her grain of salt to build psychoanalysis but also to put any convictions into question. Each analyst needs others in order to see their blind spots and alleys. These exchanges lead to a democratisation of the inter-analytic exchanges and functioning within psychoanalytic societies.

Whereas the mainstream practice of psychoanalysis is worked out individually, the policy of working groups composed of analysts from several European societies assumes the shape of a working group among colleagues opening onto new constructive perspectives.

Given that statutorily the goals of the EPF must be scientific, the EPF's actions may only be developed within the scientific sphere in order to promote analytic knowledge or the spread of psychoanalysis through increasing the contact spheres between psychoanalysis and psychoanalysts and the extra-analytic world.

The future of the EPF is prepared for today

Exposed to the cultural, scientific, social and technological changes of the societies in which our discipline was born, and very often asked about what the future holds for our practice, psychoanalysts today feel duty-bound to try and

117

identify the sticking-points which at present seem like obstacles in order to grasp the transformations that will appear in the near future.

In the introductory argument to the symposium 'Psychoanalysis in 2025', organised by the EPF in Berlin in 2014, we wrote that the liberal or neo-liberal world in which we now live has greatly changed the social situation and ties among individuals by creating a 'neuro-economic' man, and by giving birth to new tensions and new contradictions. One's sense of time has been turned upside down, problems must find a quiet solution in the external world to the detriment of the inner world; the suppression of displeasure must be immediate.

> The fall of the Berlin wall, barely twenty-five years ago, has opened our space to new cultures and new perspectives of exchanges of all kinds, from one end of Europe to the other, from Portugal to Russia. At the same time, liberalism, and even the ultra-liberalism which reigns undivided, has created a 'neuro-economic' man and has given rise to new tensions and new contradictions. The new digital technologies and their use have, for their part, modified many parameters, for instance, our relation to time, our experience of space, and the introduction of a certain virtualisation of human relations. How much weight should be accorded to live information, to the processing of data in terms of 'figures', to the replacement of narration by a digital diagram? Should we see in this a fantasy of mastery aimed at eliminating uncertainty, the unknown, the ephemeral, and the equivocal ... in an attempt, ultimately, to dissolve the very notion of the unconscious? How far do these tendencies affect research in psychoanalysis? Thus, what would be the consequences of normative procedures which, in the form of scales, standardized protocols, and the digital processing of results, would be substituted for shared assessments and experiences, for debate and argumentation? The human factor is at the heart of our exchanges: can verbal communication, not simply as the territory of the 'talking cure' but as a mode of transmission of our knowledge, however defective and insufficient it may be, be replaced in the slightest way, according to the new economic and scientific standards, by representations in figures? (Frisch, Kahn, Bleger, 2014)

Psychoanalysis continues to be attacked in the very ways it has been ever since Freud's time. Freud answered his critics by delving deeper into his discoveries concerning psychic functioning, not by bowdlerising his theory. It is important not to forget Freud's profound lesson by advocating changing psychoanalysis in function of social pressure and cultural difficulties.

On the other hand, other colleagues think that it's because it has lost its rigour that psychoanalysis has become a psychotherapy with scant appeal. By distancing themselves from Freud, analysts run the risk of developing a psychoanalysis that simplifies and even oversimplifies analytic thought insofar as it has lost its ties with metapsychology. Thus, the importance in recent years given to the object relations current, but likewise certain North American currents (see Owen Renik's self disclosure; 1998) emphasises interrelations or intersubjectivity, or even the interaction or dialogue between the patient and the analyst in the here-and-now of the session. We've thus found ourselves faced with 'intervention techniques.' The dissymmetry of the analytic situation fades, as does the principle of free-floating attention and, indeed, free association. While at times excessive, these criticisms nevertheless forcefully incite us to ponder and put into question certain so-called technical adaptations.

The EPF house

Having lost its visibility, psychoanalysis must increase its contact surfaces with the outside world. It must further re-conceptualise the institutional structures and federational structures that no longer fit the present-day needs of developing psychoanalysis in order to face the future's challenges. The EPF must increasingly become a key agent in these changes. To get there, it must give itself the means to react more quickly.

In an era when hundreds of thousands of refugees have found themselves on the roads of Europe in search of a roof, a place to call their own, it seemed indispensable to us to provide the EPF with a territorial identity, to lay down its roots. Brussels seemed appropriate to us – the 'capital' of Europe, with an international airport and low-cost flights, with quick train connections and reasonably-priced hotels but also a place where real estate was still accessible.

The EPF took the major decision of acquiring 400 square metres (some 4300 square feet) of space in Brussels, which are now available to European analysts. To what purpose? We may summarise the three principal reasons.

Without its own space, the EPF was leading a nomadic life. Each meeting had to be organised by an external agency that we had to pay. Now regular meetings – Executive meetings, the Council, the Forum on Education, the New Members Seminar, and others – can be organised there by the EPF.

Next, the idea is to have available, for the foreseeable future, a structure capable of reacting quickly to certain political and social situations, to make the voices of psychoanalysts in Europe heard. The question of a professionalising of our structures was thus indispensable, faced with the risk of continuing to work like a bunch of boy scouts.

But the principal idea was to be able to make available a fixed place to accommodate analysts keen to work together – from all countries and with any theoretical orientation. Taking into account that analysts are losing their places in universities and hospitals and, consequently, their exposure to certain pathologies, it seemed essential to us to be able to stimulate our colleagues working at times in a very isolated way in specialised centres to share their experiences and knowledge with colleagues from other countries who would mutually encourage each other to put their ideas on paper. It is fundamental that the voices of psychoanalysts continue to make themselves heard in areas 'on the margin' of the couch. We must not forget that since Freud's time, psychoanalysis has developed along its margins: child and adolescent psychoanalysis, limit pathologies, psychosis, autism and so on were great opportunities and have enriched psychoanalytic theory and technique. These advances originate in the periphery of our field of application, not its centre. Now, in all countries, there still exist psychoanalysts working with 'clinical situations of the extreme' or in unusual clinical settings compared to the classic cure. But, as in every country, very few colleagues work in these treatment environments or with these very particular patients, and bringing them together is indispensable in order to give them the opportunity to think together. If these colleagues remain isolated and do not manage to work through their practice and get to know one another, analysis becomes impoverished and locks itself away in the ivory tower of the classic cure.

Would it not also be necessary to stimulate reflection on the questions touching on new family organisations, pathologies in connection with changes in the organisation of the work world? And further, it seems to us essential to keep grounded in present-day events. For instance, analysts have everything to contribute to an understanding of terrorism and a reflection as to why certain youths born in our countries and who have grown up and attended secular schools in them opt for jihad.

The clinical advances that we may acquire by investing in these 'clinical practices on the margin' would also be very useful for demonstrating the importance of psychoanalytic thought in unusual work situations and where other therapeutic approaches enrich neither clinical knowledge nor therapeutic understanding.

It is unnecessary to emphasise that the groups made up of members from different societies can also meet on the EPF premises in order to have another look at fundamental analytic concepts or aspects of analytic technique, which has been the stepchild of psychoanalysis these last years.

Such group work is clinical research based on analytic practice, which does not require astronomical funding.

The importance of the small work groups was already acknowledged in 1976 at the Brussels meeting alluded to above and which emphasised that the 'informal meetings and conferences with a small number of psychoanalysts would be more rewarding than big congresses' (Han Groen-Prakken). We are but taking up ideas that were already put forward by our former colleagues by giving them new means to be carried out.

The EPF was built up over decades and it has experienced a new resurgence and gone through important developments each time new directions – at first glance perhaps worrying – were taken. With the acquisition of these EPF premises in Brussels, the Federation takes a new turn, essential for the future. By their decision to buy these premises, the presidents of the EPF Societies have demonstrated their confidence in psychoanalysis and their confidence in new generations of analysts. To continue to develop psychoanalysis we need new generations of pioneers, of enthusiastic young analysts!

Translated from the French by Steven Jaron, Paris

Looking at the Future of the EPF

Jorge Canestri
(EPF President Elect)

In my position as President Elect I must speak essentially of the future, of how it presents itself today, full of difficulties and problems but also of promise and projects.

It is, however, fundamental for me to underline the contributions made by all the previous Executives – particularly the one directly preceding us – which have meant that today we have a greater number of societies that make up the EPF, an increased wealth of scientific initiatives and, especially, a house (The House) where these and other initiatives can be hosted to great advantage.

The EPF, the first regional organisation in the psychoanalytic world, possesses its own special characteristics from several points of view. A very important and often-emphasised characteristic is that of concentrating on the scientific aspect, stimulating it and giving it a place in conferences, meetings of working groups and exchanges between colleagues, and encouraging all the initiatives that are progressively being taken by members and by the presidents of Societies.

I should like to continue together with all the societies and their members along a road that will stimulate the development of psychoanalysis in a region that has always been characterised by its productivity, focusing on using the EPF to exchange understanding and views.

The EPF, since its foundation but especially over the past 20 years, has proved itself to be a major influence in international psychoanalysis. Besides the good quality of the individual work of its members, a contribution to this has been a careful policy aimed at the creation of working groups (Working Parties, Ad Hoc Groups, etc), which, through projects, the creation of ad hoc methodologies and over a period of time, have been able to produce theoretical and clinical material and publications that, thanks to their quality and originality, have spread throughout the international psychoanalytical world. The achievements of the EPF during the past years have been a source of inspiration to the other two IPA regions in which some of these projects have been successfully replicated.

This explains the importance we attribute to promoting and encouraging scientific production and to the relationship between the presidents and their Societies, who are the real soul of the EPF.

We feel it is opportune to consolidate and/or create certain structures within the EPF, both from an administration point of view and from that addressed specifically to scientific production and to the relationship between us and our Societies. These structures should, in time, guarantee greater stability and continuity. However, the continuity of the structures does not imply the continuity of the people involved in them with fixed-term functions.

Having premises in Brussels – thanks to the efforts of the present Executive – will facilitate the task of the next Executive and reduce expenses, but above all it will enable us to carry out on the spot three activities that we consider essential: the New Members Seminar, the Forum on Education, and the Symposia.

The first two are well known and have existed for several years. In 2014, in Berlin, a new scientific activity was proved successfully: the Symposia. The Symposia should continue to be an area in which *to experiment an opening-up to the outside*, necessary for the survival of our discipline, as well as *giving access to an exchange with other disciplines while carefully preserving our own specificity*. We intend to promote these meetings on various different topics. Also in this case, having premises in Brussels should facilitate our task.

The administrative structures, although minimal, should help the work of the Federation, which has seen an exponential increase in the number of its component Societies and the members that they represent, as well as in its participation and exchanges in international events.

Psychoanalysis is not going through a particularly easy or luminous period at the moment. As we know, the economic crisis has increased already existing difficulties that do not depend only – or perhaps even mainly – on the economy. Psychoanalysis is under attack on various fronts and its fields of action are progressively shrinking in universities, in public health systems, in culture. We cannot exclude the responsibility of the psychoanalytical institutions themselves in contributing to this situation, although it undoubtedly varies from one country to another in the region.

It is therefore essential that the EPF let its voice be heard in Europe on all those occasions when it could be useful and pertinent. The EPF should be considered an authoritative interlocutor when such matters as the mental health of the continent's populations, immigration and the resulting traumas, the problems connected with integration and multiculturalism, with fanaticism and coexistence, etc., are being discussed. We should like to set up ad hoc working groups with an objective of study and enquiry, as well as of contact with the relevant institutions – in the first place with the European Union.

It is also important that the EPF deal with the problems deriving to its members from certain provisions of insurance companies or state institutions regarding, for instance, the payment of psychoanalytic treatment, and not only that. One of the problems experienced in all the Societies of the Federation (and in psychoanalysis internationally) concerns the increase in the average age of its members. The EPF has been dealing with this matter and has produced some relevant work. We, too, will continue to keep it at the centre of our attention.

As it has been doing for the past years, the EPF must remain close, supportive and active in the defense of its members. We propose intensifying our efforts to create a network that will allow for early intervention when this appears necessary.

Without going into details about the history of the training of analysts within the Federation, it is nonetheless useful to recall that this has been a controversial issue for a long time. Fortunately, for some time now, it has been possible to make a deeper comparison and an informed verification of the differences, quality and problems of the training programmes applied in the Societies that make up the Federation.

The Forum on Education mentioned above is one of the instruments that we can use for this purpose. We intend to give greater prominence and development to its activities.

Thanks to the pioneering activity of the Institute for Eastern Europe, the integration of countries that previously had no psychoanalytical societies, or whose training systems were sometimes unconventional, is stimulating us to study which elements we consider essential, which indispensable, and which secondary or random in the training of a good analyst.

Projects of this kind have already been undertaken and completed by working groups of the Federation and some have already been published. We believe it is necessary to increase this type of work, and to continue with the meetings between the Federation's training analysts as good opportunities for identifying and confronting the problems presented by training.

We are all aware of the change, deriving from new computer and communication technologies, in mental life and in the symbolisation processes and subjectivisation of our patients, as well as the impact that all this is having on our clinical practice – an issue that has been widely debated.

Equally important are the questions posed to our psychoanalytical comprehension by the new types of parenthood, by same sex couples, and by the development of their children. The same applies to international adoption and the problems that can derive from it.

It is our view that psychoanalysis in Europe today needs to reflect and offer suggestions regarding these matters in all their aspects. The same can be said about the role that psychoanalysis has to play in the face of those childhood and geriatric pathologies that are seriously engaging the whole community.

The 'intersections' (a word that I prefer to 'interdisciplinary') with other scientific and non-scientific disciplines can be useful and productive for psychoanalysis, as long as we keep in due consideration the need to avoid the reductionism implicit in not distinguishing between languages, methods and theoretical levels and our clinical and theoretical specificity. In this field, too, we must apply ourselves and work to contribute to manifesting our presence and authority in European culture.

In the history of the Federation, relations with the International Psychoanalytic Association have gone through ups and downs. We think it is in the interests of the Federation and of the IPA that these relations should be the best possible, in full respect of competences and differences. The IPA and the EPF, for example, have created a joint venture, collaborating financially and institutionally in the functioning of the Institute for Eastern Europe. The EPF has enriched the international psychoanalytical world through the entry into the community of new Societies.

Recently, the international relations of the EPF have been enhanced by meetings with FEPAL and NAPsaC, with reciprocal participation in their respective congresses or conferences. We believe that all this contributes to the growth of psychoanalysis, and we intend to continue in this direction.

Perhaps I have left the most difficult issue until the end, although it is no less important or urgent – an issue with which we are confronted, sometimes dramatically, by reality. I have mentioned immigration, whose intensity has increased due to conflicts of which we are all aware until it has become a mass migration. And the phenomenon of mass migration goes hand-in-hand with the manifest failure of our theories and practices regarding assimilation and cultural exchange, as well as the possibility of redeeming those masses condemned by neo-liberal capitalism to marginalisation and poverty. This failure of integration transforms important sectors of our population into easy prey for indoctrination and fanaticism. Recent episodes of terrorism have illustrated this convincingly. I think that psychoanalysts have the possibility, and the duty, to reflect on and integrate – together with other disciplines – knowledge that could be useful for confronting the problem. On the occasion of the inauguration of the House of the EPF and, I won't deny it, on the wave of emotion I felt when I saw desperate people dying together with their children in the Mediterranean, and remembering the journeys undertaken by my ancestors towards the promised land of America and my own with my family in the opposite direction to flee from the repetition of other horrors and persecutions, I suggested that we think about the meaning of Europe in this context. I will briefly repeat what I said at the time (October 2015).

Among the Societies that make up the European Federation are Australia, Israel, Lebanon, Russia, South Africa, Turkey. But can the countries of these Societies and these Societies themselves be considered European? My answer is yes, they can. Europe must not be defined according to physical criteria, for no geographer can claim to be able to state with absolute certainty the boundaries of this region. And so we can hope that in the near future other Societies can become a part of Europe.

Europe can be defined with certainty mainly as a cultural area: Europe, as Edmund Husserl and later Jorge Semprun suggested, is more of a *spiritual figure*. The idea of Europe is extra-territorial; it is the result of long centuries of clashes and amalgams, and its origins can be found in Greek rationality and in the contributions of Jews, Latins, Christians and Muslims.

Two authors: Jorge Semprun who I have already mentioned, and Edgar Morin, coincided when they wrote two books with identical titles: *Think Europe*. Morin says that:

> ... the unity and uniqueness of Europe lies precisely in its dialogic nature, namely the combination of the differences without their homogenisation, making this attitude towards difference the expression of unity. One in multiplicity, multiplicity in one.

And Semprun says that his homeland:

> ... is not the language, neither Spanish nor French; my homeland is language as a space of social communication, of linguistic invention, a possibility for representing the universe, and also of changing it ...

He repeated these words to me when, during the opening of the International Psychoanalytical Congress in Nice, and at the request of the Spanish speaking colleagues present, I asked him to speak in Spanish rather than in French. At the time he said that it was certainly possible but that the language (Spanish or French) was not important.

Europe, this *spiritual figure*, is also the land of mass emigration and of immigrations, those also in masses, which are currently the object of barbaric controversies that are bringing back old horrors and ghosts.

After having lost his university chair – significantly after he had spoken about the racial laws and the monster that was growing up in Germany and Europe – Husserl writes in his discourse:

> the crisis of European existence can only have two results: either the decline of Europe converted into something alien to its own rational sense of life, a collapse into spiritual hatred and barbarity; or else the rebirth of Europe starting from the spirit of philosophy, thanks to the heroism of reason ... The greatest danger for Europe is fatigue.

Is it possible to have forgotten so quickly what John Donne already knew when in 1624 he wrote these so often rightly quoted words:

> No man is an island, entire of itself; every man is a piece of the continent, a part of the main. If a clod be washed away by the sea, Europe is the less, as well as if a promontory were ... any man's death diminishes me, because I am involved in mankind, and therefore never send to know for whom the bell tolls; it tolls for thee.

How many refugees or emigrants have already been 'washed away by the sea'; how many have we seen – as in a recurrent and repetitive nightmare – being loaded onto train carriages, how many barbed wire fences being put up, how many borders being closed, the spreading of how many xenophobic movements! Afterwards, how many years will it take to heal the wounds or to confront the memories? Semprun was able to write *The Long Voyage* in 1963, twenty years after his journey to the concentration camp of Buchenwald, crammed inside a railway van. Years of 'voluntary oblivion' in order to survive:

> Did I have the right to live in oblivion? To live thanks to this oblivion, at its expense? The blue eyes and innocent look of the young German girl made this oblivion unbearable to me. Not only mine; the general, massive, historic oblivion of all this ancient death.

Only after the death by suicide of Primo Levi was he able to write *L'écriture ou la vie* and to try to tell about his life crossed by death, about his being a 'revenant'.

These few words of mine are to say that I firmly believe that psychoanalysis in Europe today needs to reflect and offer suggestions regarding these matters in all their aspects.

We are aware of the many difficulties afflicting psychoanalysis in this particular moment in history. But this must not hide from our eyes the many opportunities that today's world and the EPF offer us for our reflection and action.

Semprun's intervention during the 42nd IPA Congress was entitled 'The future of an illusion. The illusion of a future'. If a Buchenwald 'revenant' was able to have the illusion of a future and say that 'One can talk about the future and poets venture into it with closed eyes and fertile words ...', then I would hope that we as psychoanalysts could have something to say on the future of the voice of reason in Europe.

Appendix

EPF-Conferences[1]

1976 01 – Aix en Provence
[Different papers]
1978 02 – Estoril
The Narcissism of the Psychoanalyst
1979 03 – Wembley
Negative Therapeutic Reaction
1981 04 – Rome
Defence Mechanisms and Phantasy in the Psychoanalytical Process
1983 05 – Jerusalem
The Psychoanalytic Encounter
1985 06 – The Hague
Interpretation – of the Past or the Present?
1987 07 – Barcelona
Understanding and Interpretation of the Negative Transference
1989 08 – Heidelberg
Working Through in Psychoanalysis
1991 09 – Stockholm
Beyond Words. The significance of Non-verbal Communication in
the Psychoanalytical Process
1993 10 – Vienna
Hearing and Experiencing. The Unfolding of the Analytical Dialogue

---

1   Arranged by Peter Wegner

1995 11 – Nice
Homosexuality
1997 12 – Geneva
Borderline and Hysteria. Metapsychological
1999 13 – Berlin
Love, Hate and Violence: A Challenge to Contemporary Psychoanalysis
2001 14 – Madrid
Idols and Ideals. The Super-Ego and Ego Ideal in a World of Tur-
moil
2002 15 – Prague (The first New Style EPF Annual Conferenc)
The influence of External Reality on the Clinical Setting
2003 16 – Sorrento
The Person of the Analyst in the Psychoanalytic Cure: The Intrapsychic Paradox in Different Psychoanalytic Traditions
2004 17 – Helsinki
Present-Day Experience and Use of the Unconscious – or: Which Unconscious? And for Which Psychoanalysis?
2005 18 – Vilamoura
Interpretation and Construction in Psychoanalysis
2006 19 – Athens
Psychic Transformations in the Psychoanalytic Process
2007 20 – Barcelona
Time, Timelessness
2008 21 – Vienna
The Shadow of the Heritage
2009 22 – Brussels
Different Forms of Unconscious Communication
2010 23 – London
Passion, Love and Sexuality in Psychoanalysis
2011 24 – Kopenhagen
Anxieties and Method in Psychoanalysis
2012 25 – Paris
Initial Psychoanalytic Consultation and Treatment Process
2013 26 – Basel
Formlessness: Deformation, Transformation

2014 27 – Turin
    Ruptures
2015 28 – Stockholm
    Too much – Not enough
2016 29 – Berlin
    ¿Authority?

EPF Executives as they Appear in the Bulletins

The following tables show the EPF Executives as they appear in the Bulletins. Information between 1966 and 1972 (when the Bulletin was published for the first time) has been taken from the paper by Han Groen-Prakken on the history of the EPF, published in the Bulletin 26–27. Arranged by Glòria Estruch, February 2012.

Appendix

Years Bulletins	Honorary President	President	Vice-Presidents	Secretary	Treasurer	Editor of the Bulletin
1966 EPF creation	Anna Freud	Raymond de Saussure	J. Thiel; J. Sandler; S. Lebovici; H.E. Richter	Evelyne Kestemberg	Lois Munro	
1967–1968–1969–1970 (EPF is recognised officially by the IPA in 1969)	Anna Freud	Raymond de Saussure	probably as in 1966, but list not found			
1971	Anna Freud	Wilhelm Solms	H.P. Hildebrand; S. Lebovici; R.U. Mekking; J. Sandler; H. Thomä	Daniel Widlöcher	Lois Munro	
1972 Bull. 1	Anna Freud	Wilhelm Solms	H.P. Hildebrand; S. Lebovici; R.U. Mekking; J. Sandler; H. Thomä	Daniel Widlöcher	Lois Munro	**Editor:** H.P. Hildebrand **Editorial Board:** M. de M'Uzan; S. Stephanos; D. Widlöcher
1973 Bull. 2, 3	Anna Freud	Wilhelm Solms	H.P. Hildebrand; S. Lebovici; R.U. Mekking; J. Sandler; H. Thomä	Daniel Widlöcher/ J.-B. Pontalis	Lois Munro	**Editor:** H.P. Hildebrand **Editorial Board:** M. de M'Uzan; S. Stephanos; D. Widlöcher
1974 Bull. 4	Anna Freud	Wilhelm Solms	H.P. Hildebrand; M. de M'Uzan; J. Sandler; J. de Saussure; V. Tähkä; L. Zaccaria-Gairinger	J.-B. Pontalis	R.U. Mekking	**Editor:** H.P. Hildebrand **Editorial Board:** M. de M'Uzan; S. Stephanos; J.-B. Pontalis
1974 Bull. 5 – Glossary	Anna Freud	Wilhelm Solms	H.P. Hildebrand; M. de M'Uzan; J. Sandler; J. de Saussure; V. Tähkä; L. Zaccaria-Gairinger	J.-B. Pontalis	R.U. Mekking	**Editor:** H.P. Hildebrand **Editorial Board:** M. de M'Uzan; S. Stephanos; D. Widlöcher
1975 Bull. 6	Anna Freud	Wilhelm Solms	H.P. Hildebrand; M. de M'Uzan; J. Sandler; J. de Saussure; V. Tähkä; L. Zaccaria-Gairinger	J.-B. Pontalis	R.U. Mekking	**Editor:** H.P. Hildebrand **Editorial Board:** M. de M'Uzan; S. Stephanos; J.-B. Pontalis
1976–1977 Bull. 7, 8, 9, 10, 11	Anna Freud	Joseph Sandler	J. Chasseguet-Smirgel; J. de Saussure; E. Gaddini; V. Tähkä; P.H. Hildebrand	Alex Holder	R.U. Mekking	**Editor:** H.P. Hildebrand **Editorial Board:** A. Holder; R. Major; A. Rilton; V. Smirnoff, S. Stephanos
1977–1978 Bull. 12, 13	Anna Freud	Joseph Sandler	J. Chasseguet-Smirgel; A. Pollock; J. de Saussure; V. Tähkä; E. Moersch	Alex Holder	R.U. Mekking	Daniel Widlöcher

Years Bulletins	Honorary President	President	Vice-Presidents	Secretary	Treasurer	Editor of the Bulletin
1979	Anna Freud	Joseph Sandler/ Daniel Widlöcher	J. Chasseguet-Smirgel; A. Pollock; J. de Saussure; V. Tähkä; E. Moersch/ André Haynal; Anne-Marie Sandler	Alex Holder/ Gemma Jappe	R.U. Mekking/ Alex Pollock	Daniel Widlöcher/ Daniel Widlöcher
1980 Bull. 14	Anna Freud	Daniel Widlöcher	André Haynal Anne-Marie Sandler	Gemma Jappe	Alex Pollock	Daniel Widlöcher
1980 Bull. 15	Anna Freud	Daniel Widlöcher	André Haynal Anne-Marie Sandler	Gemma Jappe	Alex Pollock	Terttu Eskelinen de Folch
1981-1982 Bull. 16, 17, 18, 19 & 1st Monograph on Training	Anna Freud	Daniel Widlöcher	André Haynal Anne-Marie Sandler	Gemma Jappe	Alex Pollock	Terttu Eskelinen de Folch
1983-1984-1985 Bull. 20-21, 22, 23, 24		Anne-Marie Sandler	André Haynal Heinz Henseler	Alain Gibeault	Alex Pollock	Terttu Eskelinen de Folch
1985-1986-1987 Bull. 25, 26-27, 28		Anne-Marie Sandler	Heinz Henseler Han Groen-Prakken	Alain Gibeault	René Fischer	Terttu Eskelinen de Folch
1987 Bull. 29		Han Groen-Prakken	Heinz Henseler Alain Gibeault	Ronald Baker	René Fischer	Terttu Eskelinen de Folch
1988-1989 Bull. 30, 31, 32, 33		Han Groen-Prakken	Heinz Henseler Alain Gibeault	Ronald Baker	René Fischer	Alex Holder
1990-1991 Bull. 34, 35, 36		Han Groen-Prakken	Terttu Eskelinen de Folch; Alain Gibeault	Ronald Baker	René Fischer	Alex Holder
1991-1992-1993 Bull. 37, 38, 39, 40		Terttu Eskelinen de Folch	Alain Gibeault James Innes-Smith	Lars Sjögren	Alex Pollock	Alex Holder
1993-1994-1995 Bull. 41, 42, 43, 44 & 2nd Monograph on Training		Terttu Eskelinen de Folch	Henk Jan Dalewijk James Innes-Smith	Lars Sjögren	Alex Pollock	Alex Holder
1995-1996 Bull. 45, 46		Alain Gibeault	Henk Jan Dalewijk James Innes-Smith	Betty Denzler	Alex Pollock	Alex Holder
1996-1997 Bull. 47, 48		Alain Gibeault	James Innes-Smith Henk Jan Dalewijk	Betty Denzler	Alex Pollock	Gabriele Junkers
1997-1998-1999 Bull. 49, 50, 51, 52, 53 & Glossary		Alain Gibeault	Emma Piccioli Imre Szecsödy	Betty Denzler	Henk Jan Dalewijk	Gabriele Junkers
2000 Bull. 54		David Tuckett	Emma Piccioli Imre Szecsödy	Gabriele Junkers	Henk Jan Dalewijk	Eike Wolff

Years Bulletins	Honorary President	President	Vice-Presidents	Secretary	Treasurer	Editor of the Bulletin
2001–2002 Bull. 55, 56		David Tuckett	Yolanda Gampel Evelyne Séchaud	Gabriele Junkers	Henk Jan Dalewijk	Eike Wolff
2003 Bull. 57		David Tuckett	Yolanda Gampel Evelyne Séchaud	Gabriele Junkers	Duveken Engels	Eike Wolff
2004 Bull. 58		Evelyne Séchaud	Yolanda Gampel Vincenzo Bonaminio	Anna Danielsson Berglund	Duveken Engels	Jordi Sala
2005 Bull. 59		Evelyne Séchaud	Vincenzo Bonaminio Gigliola Fornari Spoto	Anna Danielsson Berglund	Duveken Engels	Jordi Sala
2006 Bull. 60		Evelyne Séchaud	Vincenzo Bonaminio Peter Wegner	Anna Danielsson Berglund	Duveken Engels	Jordi Sala
2007 Bull. 61		Evelyne Séchaud	Vincenzo Bonaminio Peter Wegner	Anna Danielsson Berglund	Duveken Engels	Jordi Sala
2008 Bull. 62		Peter Wegner	Ronny Jaffè Jonathan Sklar	Judit Meszaros	Duveken Engels	Dieter Bürgin
2009 Bull. 63		Peter Wegner	Ronny Jaffè Jonathan Sklar	Denny Panitz	Anne Rosenberg	Dieter Bürgin
2010 Bull. 64		Peter Wegner	Ronny Jaffè Jonathan Sklar	Denny Panitz	Anne Rosenberg	Dieter Bürgin
2011 Bull. 65		Peter Wegner	Ronny Jaffè Jonathan Sklar	Denny Panitz	Anne Rosenberg	Dieter Bürgin
2012 Bull. 66		Serge Frisch	Eva Schmid-Gloor Franziska Ylander	Leopoldo Bleger	Anne Rosenberg	Ursula Burkert
2013 Bull. 67		Serge Frisch	Eva Schmid-Gloor Franziska Ylander	Leopoldo Bleger	Alexander Janssen	Ursula Burkert
2014 Bull. 68		Serge Frisch	Eva Schmid-Gloor Franziska Ylander	Leopoldo Bleger	Alexander Janssen	Ursula Burkert
2015 Bull. 68		Serge Frisch	Eva Schmid-Gloor Franziska Ylander	Leopoldo Bleger	Alexander Janssen	Ursula Burkert

About the Authors

Jorge Canestri, Prof., M.D., psychiatrist, psychoanalyst, training and supervising analyst for the Italian Psychoanalytical Association (A.I.Psi), full member of the Argentine Psychoanalytic Association (APA). Full Member of the International Psychoanalytic Association. Mary S. Sigourney Award recipient 2004. Chair of the 42nd Congress of the International Psychoanalytic Association (IPA) in Nice (2001). Associate Editor for Europe of the International Journal of Psycho-Analysis. Member of the Editorial Board of "Aperturas Psicoanalíticas", Member of the Editorial Board of Psychoanalytic Psychotherapy, Director of the webpage: Psychoanalysis and logical mathematical thought, Member of the Advisory Board of Philoctete, New York, USA IPA global representative for Europe from 2005 to 2007 and representative for Europe to the IPA Executive Committee from 2007 to 2009. Chair of the Working Party on Theoretical Issues of the European Psychoanalytical Federation until 2010; and Chair of the IPA's International New Groups Committee until 2012. President Elect of the European Psychoanalytical Federation 2015. He has published numerous psychoanalytical papers and numerous books.

Serge Frisch, M.D., psychiatrist, training analyst, Belgian Psychoanalytic Society. President of the EPF (2012–2016), general secretary (2006–2008) and president (2008–2012) of the Belgian Psychoanalytic Society. Chair of the EPF working party The Specificity of the Psychoanalytic Treatment Today (2009–2012). Member of the IPA sponsoring committee to the Beirut

Psychoanalytic Association (ALdeP). Member of the IPA committee Psycho-analysis and Allied Professions (2001–2005). Vice-chair of the IPA Outreach committee (2009–2011). President of the European Federation for Psycho-analytic Psychotherapy (1996–2002), Member of the Board of Advisors of the Helix Centre For Interdisciplinary Investigation, New York. Member of the Editiorial Board of L'année Psychanalytique Internationale (2005–2008).

Alain Gibeault, Ph.D., is a Training Analyst of the Paris Psychoanalytical Society. He has played an important role on the international scene as President of the European Psycho-Analytical Federation from 1995 to 1999 and as Past Secretary General of the International Psychoanalytical Association from 2001 to 2003. He was Director of the E. & J. Kestemberg Centre for Psycho-analysis and Psychotherapy (Mental Health Association of Paris 13th) from 1997 to 2014. He has published with Dana Birksted-Breen and Sara Flanders an anthology of French psychoanalytic papers entitled *Reading French Psychoanalysis* (Routledge, 2010) and a book entitled *Chemins de la symbolisation* (Presses Universitaires de France, 2010). As a Member of the EPF Working Party on Initiating Psychoanalysis, he was one of the contributors of the book on first interviews entitled *Initiating Psychoanalysis. Perspectives* (Routledge, 2012).

Han Groen-Prakken (1927–2003), M.D., member of the NVPA in the Netherlands and later president of this society. 1982–87 member of the EPF Executive, 1987–1991 president EPF. In 1991 she founded the East European Institute, where she was an active member until her death. In 2002 her work in this field was honoured by naming this pioneering EPF/IPA venture "Han Groen-Prakken Psychoanalytic Institute for Eastern Europe". She has published extensively in psychoanalysis.

Anne-Marie Sandler was born in Geneva, studied with Jean Piaget and was for a time his assistant. She then came to England, where she trained in child analysis with Anna Freud, going on to complete the adult training in the British Psychoanalytical Society, where she is a training and supervising analyst, working with adults and children. She has been President of the British Society and of the European Psychoanalytical Federation, and Vice President of the International Psychoanalytical Association. She was formerly Director of the Anna Freud Centre. She published a number of papers, amongst them *The Structure of Transference Interpretations in Clinical Practice* (1985) and '*Aspects of the Analysis of a Neurotic Patient*' (1988). A few further papers like *Psychoanalytic Technique and Theory of Psychic Change* (1992) and *The Past Unconscious and the Present Unconscious, a contribution to a technical frame of reference* (1994), were written in collaboration with Joseph Sandler. They also collaborated on a book, *Internal Objects Revisited*, published in 1998.

Eva Schmid-Gloor, psychoanalyst in private practice in Zürich (Switzerland), training analyst of the Swiss Society of Psychoanalysis. In the past president of the Freud Institute in Zürich, vice president of the Swiss Society of Psychoanalysis, chair of the training committee of the Swiss Society of Psychoanalysis. Since 2011 Vice President of the European Psychoanalytic Federation. She teaches since 1996 regularly at the Freud Institute in Zürich and recently to several groups in various German Psychoanalytic Institutes. Thematic interests: psychoanalytic technique, transgenerational issues, psychosomatics.

Evelyne Sechaud, training and supervising analyst at the French Psychoanalytic Association (APF). She was President and Director of the Institute of the APF 1999–2001 and President of the EPF 2003–2007. During her mandate she created the Working Party *Specificity of the psychoanalytic treatment today*. In the EPF she has also taken part in the Forum on Education and presented the French model of Education. She has published many papers mainly about transference, psychoanalytic technique and sublimation.

David Tuckett is a training and supervising Analyst of the British Psychoanalytic Society, former Editor in Chief of the International Journal of Psychoanalysis (1988–2001), Joint Executive Director of Psychoanalytic Electronic Publishing and Professor and Director of the Centre for the Study of Decision-Making Uncertainty at University College London. He was Chair of the EPF Working Party on Comparative Clinical Methods (2002–2011) and won the Sigourney Prize in 2007.

Peter Wegner, Dr. rer. soc., Dipl.-Psych., is a training and supervising analyst of the German Psychoanalytical Association, since 1995 in private practice in Tübingen, Southwest Germany. He is born 1952 in Berlin and studied Psychology from 1972 to 1978 at the University of Tübingen, followed by a training in Psychodrama (1982) and Psychoanalysis (1986). From 1978 to 1982 he was employee at two centers for counseling (children/adults) and from 1982 to 1995 assistant lecturer at the Department for Psychoanalysis, Psychotherapy and Psychosomatic, University of Tübingen (Medical Director Prof. Dr. med. H. Henseler). He was chair of the training committee of the Institute for Psychoanalysis Stuttgart/Tübingen (2000–2006) and member of the Publication Committee of the IPA (2001–2005). He was Vice-President (2006–2008) and President (2008–2012) of the European Psychoanalytical Federation (EPF). He has specialized on clinical questions of long-term and high frequent psychoanalysis with numerous published papers in this field. See all publications under www.drpeterwegner.de).

Daniel Widlöcher, born in 1929, has parallel to his psychoanalytic investment pursued a quite important carrier in psychiatry, at university and as a researcher. He was one of the founders of the Association Psychanalytique de France in 1964, twice it's President, President also of the European Psychoanalytical Federation (1979–1983) and of the International Psychoanalytical Association (2001–2005). Among his important theoretical and clinical contributions, we can highlight *Métapsychologie du sens* [Metapsychology of the sense (meaning)] (1986) and *Les Nouvelles Cartes de la Psychanalyse* [The new cards of psychoanalysis] (1996). He is also the author of a memoir: *Comment on devient psychanalyste ... et comment on le reste* [How to become an analyst ... and how to stay it] (2010).

www.ingramcontent.com/pod-product-compliance
Lightning Source LLC
Chambersburg PA
CBHW020707270326
41928CB00005B/309